A FALCON GUIDE®

Cave Exp

The Definitive Guide to Caving Technique, Safety, Gear, and Trip Leadership

PAUL BURGER

FALCON GUIDE®

GUILFORD, CONNECTICUT
HELENA, MONTANA

AN IMPRINT OF THE GLOBE PEQUOT PRESS

Illustrations © by Paul Burger
Text design by Nancy Freeborn

Library of Congress Cataloging-in-Publication Data
Burger, Paul.
    Cave exploring : the definitive guide to caving technique, safety, gear, and trip leadership / Paul Burger. — 1st ed.
        p. cm. — (Falcon guide)
    Includes index.
    ISBN–13: 978-0-7627-2560-1
    ISBN–10: 0-7627-2560-5
    1. Caving. 2. Caving—Equipment and supplies. I. Title. II. Series.
GV200.62.B87 2006
796.52′5—dc22

                                                            2005035913

Manufactured in the United States of America
First Edition/First Printing

Warning: Cave exploring is a dangerous sport. You can be seriously injured or die. Read the following before you use this book.

This is an instruction book about cave exploring, an activity that is inherently dangerous. Do not depend solely on information from this book for your personal safety. Your safety depends on your own judgment based on competent instruction, experience, and a realistic assessment of your ability.

The training and other advice given in this book are the author's opinions. Consult your physician before engaging in any part of the training program described by the author.

There are no warranties, either expressed or implied, that this instruction book contains accurate and reliable information. There are no warranties as to fitness for a particular purpose or that this book is merchantable. Your use of this book indicates your assumption of the risk of death or serious injury as a result of cave exploring's risks and is an acknowledgment of your own sole responsibility for your safety in cave exploring or in training for the activity.

The Globe Pequot Press assumes no liability for accidents happening to, or injuries sustained by, readers who engage in the activities described in this book.

Contents

Acknowledgments

This type of book requires collaboration and would not have been possible without the help and advice of other experts. I would like to thank Stan Allison, Larry Fish, Joanne Greenberg, Rob Lee, Dr. Stephen Mosberg, and Pat Seiser for their invaluable reviews and suggestions. Many of my caving friends provided photographs and acted as models to help illustrate some of the techniques in the book; thanks to Stan Allison, Hazel Barton, Amy Bern, Carl Bern, Dayna DeFeo, Kevin Downey, Jeff Goben, Rob Lee, Steve Lester, Rob Lorenz, and Steve Reames. Special thanks goes to those people who taught me how to safely explore caves, explained how to map caves, and inspired me with the drive to see what was around the next corner: Donald Davis, Don Doucette, Larry Fish, Dave Harris, Pat Kambesis, Fred Luiszer, Stu Marlatt, Steve Reames, Rick Rhinehart, Steve and Lisa Shertz, and Todd Warren. Finally, I'd like to thank my parents, Douglass Burger and Susan Morgan, for the encouragement and support during my formative caving years despite the tracked-in mud, overdue arrivals, and requests for gas money.

An Introduction to Caving

Caving, like any other athletic activity, is best learned through practice. The purpose of this book is to teach you basic caving skills in an easy-to-follow manner, and to keep you from making some of the mistakes almost all of us made as novice cavers. The information here will help you select gear, from the right cave packs, helmets, and lights to the right clothes. This book covers many different types of caves, from dry, horizontal maze caves to deep, vertical, wet caves. It will teach you techniques to explore them safely and with minimal impact. Hopefully you will also come away from this book with an understanding of this unique underground world and what makes caves such excellent resources for recreation, exploration, and science.

Before we go any further, a quick word on terminology: You will hear many different terms for "caver," including *spelunker*, *speleologist*, or just *cave explorer*. Despite what many experienced cavers will say, *caver* and *spelunker* mean the same thing: someone who explores caves. Many cavers in the United States use the term *spelunker* as a derogatory label for people who go into caves intent on vandalism or are just plain unprepared.

The label *speleologist* describes someone who goes into caves for scientific purposes. The use of this term is slowly going out of vogue, and you will rarely hear cave scientists refer to themselves as speleologists—even though it is a pretty cool word.

CAVING STYLES

Because caves differ throughout the United States, you will find caving groups using slightly different techniques. U.S. and European equipment and techniques, especially vertical caving methods, have developed largely independently from each other. Recently, however, the two styles have begun to merge, with cavers taking the best of both styles. The caving styles, gear, and techniques in this book are those currently used by U.S. cavers with limited mention of those common only to Europe.

TYPES OF CAVES

A *cave* is any natural opening in bedrock large enough for a human to fit into that reaches total darkness. Contrary to what is often stated in the media, human-made features such as mines, tunnels, and storm sewers are not caves. This book will help you learn to explore caves safely, but it will not teach you the skills you need to safely enter a mine. Mines are much more dangerous and require different skills and judgments. Caves are formed naturally and have had thousands or millions of years to stabilize, while most mines have only been open for a couple of centuries. Mine roofs are supported by old timbers and beams that can deteriorate, leaving the ceiling unstable. Debris on mine floors can hide shafts and other hazards. Simply put, stay out of mines and mine shafts, underground quarries, abandoned missile silos, or any other human-made underground feature that is no longer maintained.

Solution or Epigenic Caves

Most caves are *epigenic caves*, created by water slowly dissolving some kind of soluble bedrock—usually limestone, but sometimes gypsum or salt. Rainwater picks up carbon

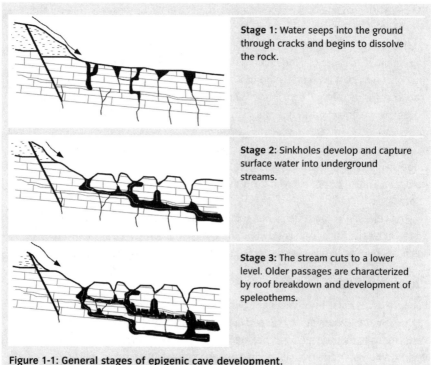

Stage 1: Water seeps into the ground through cracks and begins to dissolve the rock.

Stage 2: Sinkholes develop and capture surface water into underground streams.

Stage 3: The stream cuts to a lower level. Older passages are characterized by roof breakdown and development of speleothems.

Figure 1-1: General stages of epigenic cave development.

dioxide from the atmosphere and soil, creating a weak carbonic acid. This acid seeps into cracks and begins to dissolve the bedrock. As the openings became wider, more water is able to get into the rock, and the process of dissolution is accelerated. Eventually the water flowing through different cracks joins, forming underground streams and rivers. As this type of cave matures, it captures nearly all of the water that falls on the surface, leaving dry streambeds and sinkholes, and carries the water underground where it eventually resurfaces as springs.

Hypogenic Caves

Some caves, such as the caves of the Black Hills in South Dakota and the Guadalupe Mountains in New Mexico, are formed below the water table where two different types

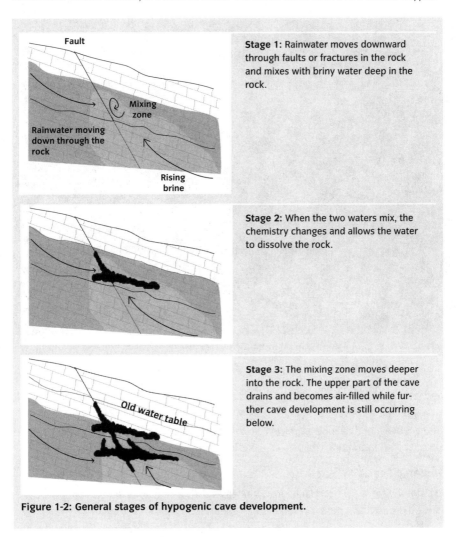

Stage 1: Rainwater moves downward through faults or fractures in the rock and mixes with briny water deep in the rock.

Stage 2: When the two waters mix, the chemistry changes and allows the water to dissolve the rock.

Stage 3: The mixing zone moves deeper into the rock. The upper part of the cave drains and becomes air-filled while further cave development is still occurring below.

Figure 1-2: General stages of hypogenic cave development.

of waters mixed. The mixing causes the water to be more chemically active, which makes it dissolve the rock more easily. These *hypogenic caves* are not characterized by sinkholes or cave springs; they are usually dry except for some areas of dripping or where they reach the local water table. Hypogenic caves are usually extensive mazes or complex networks that resemble the inside of a sponge.

Lava Tubes

As lava flows downhill, those parts of the flow in contact with the air or underlying rock cool relatively quickly, creating a solid tube, while the interior of the flow is still molten. The molten lava will continue to flow and sometimes drain out of the tube, leaving behind a *lava tube cave*. You can find lava tube caves throughout the Pacific Northwest

A lava tube cave in El Malpais National Monument, New Mexico. PHOTO BY PAUL BURGER

and Northern California, New Mexico, and Hawaii. Lava tubes can range from short individual segments to very complex mazes of overlapping and intersecting passages. One of the longest and deepest caves in the United States is a lava tube cave system in Hawaii called Kazumura, which is 41 miles long and more than 3,600 feet deep.

Tectonic Caves

Tectonic caves, also called fault caves, are essentially cracks or openings in bedrock caused by faulting, erosion, or other processes that do not involve solution. These caves are generally found in rocks such as granite, gneiss, and even volcanic tuff. You don't find many cave decorations in tectonic caves, but they can be beautiful, complex, and a great deal of fun to explore. Many tectonic caves are formed as large blocks of rock slide downward toward the bottom of a canyon, leaving cracks in the bedrock. In some cases, large blocks will slide to the bottom of a canyon, bridging over a stream, and form a tectonic stream cave. Stream erosion will make the cave passage larger, and continued rockfall will make the roof thicker. Eventually the cave roof becomes thick enough to support vegetation and looks the same as the surrounding bedrock.

Boulder Caves

Boulder caves or talus caves form within large piles of rock where the voids in between leave enough space for a person to fit through. Many boulder caves are found where rocks have fallen into a stream valley and water has carried smaller rocks and sediment away. These caves are often unstable, and even the most heavily visited boulder caves are subject to occasional shifting rock. Be very careful in this type of cave.

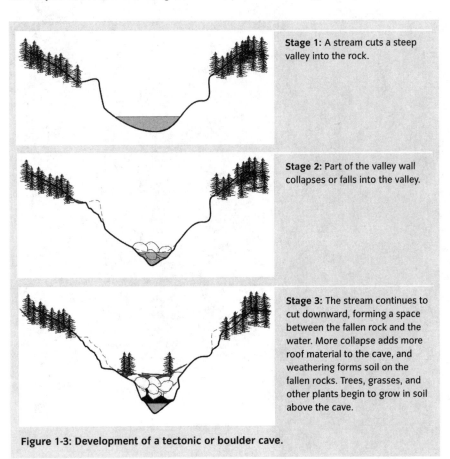

Stage 1: A stream cuts a steep valley into the rock.

Stage 2: Part of the valley wall collapses or falls into the valley.

Stage 3: The stream continues to cut downward, forming a space between the fallen rock and the water. More collapse adds more roof material to the cave, and weathering forms soil on the fallen rocks. Trees, grasses, and other plants begin to grow in soil above the cave.

Figure 1-3: Development of a tectonic or boulder cave.

[above] A granite tectonic cave in Colorado.
PHOTO BY PAUL BURGER [left] A granite boulder cave in
Colorado. PHOTO BY CARLETON BERN

SPELEOTHEMS

Most limestone caves will have various kinds of speleothems, also called cave formations or decorations.

Calcite Speleothems

As water moves through fractures and pores in limestone and dissolves the rock, it picks up calcium carbonate (also called calcite). When this water reaches an air-filled cave passage, it deposits a little of the calcite. Over many eons, these small deposits can create large formations.

Columns, stalactites, and stalagmites. COURTESY NATIONAL PARK SERVICE, PHOTO BY PETER JONES

The formations that hang from the ceiling are called *stalactites*, and those that build up from the floor are called *stalagmites*. When a stalactite and stalagmite grow together, it is called a *column*. If the water coming into the cave flows along the walls or floor in a sheet instead of dripping, the calcite is deposited in thin layers like a frozen waterfall called *flowstone*.

Formations can build up around the edges of cave pools. A thin layer of calcium carbonate builds up at the edge because evaporation is higher. This layer can eventually build higher, damming the flow and keeping water from flowing past. A new layer of calcite will form at this level, and through this process create *rimstone dams* that can be anywhere from a few inches to several feet high.

You will sometimes see a knobby growth in the cave that resembles cauliflower or popcorn. *Cave popcorn* is formed when water splashes onto the wall after hitting the floor or a stalagmite, or as water seeps out of tiny pores. The small drops of water on the wall evaporate, leaving behind calcite and creating irregular bulbous shapes.

Some water seeping through pores in the wall is under pressure due to the force of gravity on the water in the rock above. As the water is forced out of the wall, it deposits calcite, but because it's under pressure it can grow upward or sideways. Formations that grow under these conditions are called *helictites* and frequently resemble worms or snakes coming out of the wall or even out of other formations.

Cave popcorn in Carlsbad Cavern. PHOTO BY CARLETON BERN

Helictites in a Colorado cave. PHOTO BY CARLETON BERN

Gypsum Speleothems

Calcite isn't the only mineral that can be found in a cave, though it's the most common. Many caves also have trace amounts of calcium sulfate or gypsum. Gypsum is much more easily dissolved than calcite and is easier to deposit. Small amounts of gypsum in cave sediments can actually grow new crystals in the humid cave environment. In some caves you may only see a slight sparkle of gypsum in the sediment or cave walls, but in others you can see large crystals.

Some crystals, called gypsum flowers, will form thick curves that appear to grow as if they were squeezed out like toothpaste. Others will form long, narrow individual crystals called gypsum needles. In caves containing quite a bit of gypsum, you may find gypsum chandeliers made of crystals that can grow from just a few inches to more than 10 feet long.

Gypsum flowers in a Wyoming cave. PHOTO BY CARLETON BERN

CAVE BIOLOGY

There are three basic zones to a cave environment: the entrance, the twilight zone, and complete darkness. You will find different types of cave life in each of these zones. Plants are rarely found beyond the entrance and you may see some algae growing in the twilight zone, but most cave life consists of vertebrates, invertebrates, and microbes. For simplicity, I will refer to all of these as animals.

Some animals are found primarily in entrance zones, including snakes, spiders, birds, mountain lions, and the occasional sheep or other livestock. These animals use caves as temporary shelters or as nesting sites, but are not true cave dwellers.

Trogloxenes are animals that frequently use caves but must return to the surface for food or other needs. Some mammals, such as many species of bats, use caves as their primary residence, but to survive must venture out each night to feed on insects, plant nectar, or other animals. Other trogloxenes include frogs, salamanders, pack rats, ring-tail cats, raccoons, and cave swallows.

Troglophiles are animals that prefer environments like caves but can survive outside if suitable habitat exists. Insects such as cave crickets, some crustaceans like crayfish, many types of microbes, and even some fish that live in springs are considered troglophiles.

Troglobites are true cave dwellers that are adapted to and complete their life cycle in the total darkness of a cave. Fish and salamanders are the only common vertebrates with relatives that have adapted to the cave environment. Fully cave adapted fish and salamanders are usually blind and have very slow metabolisms in order to survive in an environment with much less food than on the surface. The majority of troglobites are

A cave cricket in Carlsbad Cavern.
PHOTO BY DR. JEAN K. KREJCA, ZARA ENVIRON-
MENTAL LLC

invertebrates like crickets and other insects, spring-tails, arachnids, blind crayfish, and microbes.

Microbes are by far the most diverse group of troglobitic organisms found in caves. While some are obviously related to microbes found on the surface and in the soil and rock, others are unique to caves. Some of these microbes live in underground pools, and some live on the walls and ceiling. They use impurities in the rock such as iron and manganese as a food source.

Though you cannot see them, their presence can be detected if you know what to look for. Sometimes microbes can cause water to bead up on the surface of the rock and look like spots of gold or silver. In other cases microbes can leave deposits of oxidized iron or manganese on the walls up to several inches thick.

WHY ARE CAVES IMPORTANT?

If you have picked up this book, you probably have some curiosity about caves and what the underground world is like. Most cavers, including most cave scientists, began caving for fun and adventure. Caves do offer excellent challenges and experiences to those who learn to explore safely, but there are other mysteries beyond knowing what's around the next corner. Caves can help to answer many questions about not only what is going on today, but what has gone on in the past as well.

Areas with abundant caves, sinkholes, and springs are called *karst* areas. Karst regions are characterized by very little flowing water on the surface even though the rainfall may be high. Twenty percent of the land area in the United States is classified as karst. People in these areas get most of their drinking water from water tables fed by caves. Places such as Austin, Texas, Bowling Green, Kentucky, and most of Florida depend on caves and karst springs for water.

Every surface activity has an impact on the water below, especially since caves tend to act like pipes that quickly carry contamination long distances. In many karst areas you will see people using sinkholes as dumps for garbage or as places to direct effluent from sewage treatment and other facilities. These sinkholes lead to cave passages and eventually to the groundwater or to springs feeding surface streams, rivers, and lakes.

A more subtle, yet no less harmful pollution comes from overall land use and practices. Agriculture, even lawn fertilizing, puts pollutants into the water. Runoff from pavement carries oil, heavy metals, and other chemicals into the groundwater. How many times have you seen people washing their cars or gas station owners hosing down pavement with water and allowing it to run into storm drains? The net effect of all these activities is pollution of groundwater and water supplies.

Caves and springs have been used not only by modern people, but by Native Americans as well. Indians explored caves, used them for shelter and as water sources, and in some cases mined gypsum and other salts from them for medicinal purposes. Some caves were and still are major religious sites. All of this activity has left behind artifacts that can help archaeologists piece together what life was like hundreds and thousands of years ago. Since caves shelter these artifacts from destruction by weather and activities such as construction, they can sometimes harbor the only known evidence of people who lived in an area thousands of years ago. This is why it's important to leave any archaeological materials you may find in place: so future researchers and cavers can see them in their correct context.

Caves not only supply shelter and water for us, but also provide habitat for many species of animals. As noted, different animals use various areas within a cave, and some require the cave environment to survive. This was true in the past as well. Animals such as the extinct short-faced bear and ground sloth have left their scat, nests, scratches, and even bones in caves. By looking at layers of bones and other deposits, it's possible to discover what plants and animals lived in the area and even what the climate was like.

Cave formations can provide information on past climate and may help us figure out how our climate may change in the future. During wetter times, formations tend to grow more rapidly and can have slightly different chemistry. Scientists can examine cave formations and measure the chemical makeup of the rock to determine what the climate was like far into the past.

Caves may also give us some insight into potential life on other planets. Mars has vast areas covered with volcanic basalt. Recent images have shown some features that strongly resemble the lava tube caves found here on earth. Researchers are studying lava tube caves in Hawaii to see what kind of organisms are thriving and how they evolve. They hope to use this knowledge to understand what kind of life there may be in Martian caves and how to look for life there without a human going into them.

Mars also contains large amounts of iron and manganese, but no detectable organic matter from plants and animals, so life-forms in the soil and rock would have to use these minerals as their food source. Microbes that feed on iron and manganese have been found in several caves in New Mexico and other places. These caves, like Mars, have almost no organic matter and receive no sunlight. Researchers are looking at these microbes and the materials they leave behind as analogs to what may be found in the Martian rocks and soil.

The microbes found in the deep, organic-poor caves may also provide a clue to helping cure human diseases. Because the food supply is so scarce in these caves, microbes have to fiercely compete for whatever they can get. To do this, they produce enzymes to kill off the competition. Microbiologists can sample these microbes and the enzymes they produce to see how they react with other cells, such as those that cause cancer or HIV. Some of the microbes taken out of one cave in New Mexico produce an enzyme that attacks and kills leukemia cells but leaves healthy cells behind. Of course that doesn't mean you could just go into the cave, drink some of the water, and be cured, but it does mean microbiologists can try to isolate the enzyme and develop it into a useful treatment.

People can have a tremendous impact on these microbes. As you move through a cave, you shed thousands of skin and hair cells as well as lint from your clothing. Along with these cells, you are shedding microbes that can use these cells as food. When the foreign cells and microbes are introduced into the cave environment, they take energy out of the system and can upset the natural balance. When researchers looked at several of the pools in Lechuguilla Cave, New Mexico, they discovered after only a handful of visits by highly trained and careful cavers, many of the native microbes were no longer present.

Caves are important to us as areas to explore and discover, and are important to many animals for survival. Caves are equally important for exploring the past, from climate to extinct life and vanished cultures. Caves may also offer glimpses into the future, helping us discover life on other worlds and how to save lives here on earth.

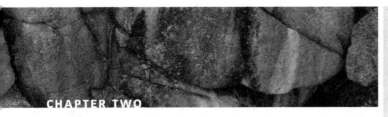

CHAPTER TWO

Caving Basics

You may have already visited a cave—perhaps a show cave, a local hangout cave, or maybe even a wild caving tour. Since you have picked up this book, you may have been already bitten by the cave bug and yearn to do more. Now comes one of the most frustrating parts of getting into caving: dealing with established cavers.

GETTING INTO CAVING

Cavers are very protective about caves, not because they want to keep them to themselves, but because uninformed people going into caves have accidentally or, more sadly, purposely caused damage. Cavers worry about cave locations becoming known to cave vandals and also worry about people getting hurt in caves. Because of this, they may be distrustful—even paranoid—about newcomers.

However, this is no reason to avoid organized cavers and just venture out on your own. If you do, you will be missing out on a great deal of valuable experience, and probably on a large number of caves you would not have access to otherwise. Once you're established, the caving community is a broad, supportive group, and you will find them willing to help you out wherever you move to in your caving career.

So where do you begin? At the end of this book, I have listed resources to help you find caving groups in your area. If you live in a heavily populated region such as the East Coast, you will find several caving groups in your area. Go to some meetings and see what kind of training trips or other training they offer. If one group does not seem to welcome newcomers or offer training trips, try a different group. Although there may not be an open trip the first weekend after the meeting you attend, ask someone for a calendar of upcoming events. Just by asking, you are showing an interest.

If none of the groups near you seems friendly or offers training trips, be persistent. Attend several meetings of the group nearest to you and listen to the caving trip reports to see who is actively working on projects. After a few meetings you should get a good idea as to who is active and who may need some help on projects.

WORKING WITH ESTABLISHED CAVERS

Be patient.

Do not overrepresent your skills or abilities.

Ask questions, but don't be pushy.

Sign up for any trip that is available, even if it's only a cave cleanup or other work trip; this will help you get to know the cavers and help them get to know you.

If you can, attend the meetings of multiple groups to increase your chances of getting on a cave trip. Cavers also have regional and national caving get-togethers several times a year. These are excellent places to go caving and get to know people.

Once you do get on a trip, pay attention to the trip leader and ask questions. As a leader of dozens of training trips, I tend to remember the people who seem eager to learn more about caves and caving, and I am much more likely to seek them out to take them underground again.

FOLLOW THE LEADER:
TIPS FOR MAKING A GOOD IMPRESSION AND GAINING SKILLS

Listen to the trip leader for guidelines for the cave you're visiting, tips on how to get past an obstacle, and any other information she may be willing to talk about.

Ask questions, but not just for the sake of asking questions.

Pay attention to how the experienced cavers move through the cave.

Keep a positive attitude no matter what happens.

Thank the trip leader for his time and ask if he plans to lead other trips in the future.

If you follow all these tips and suggestions, you will be well on your way to exploring caves and working on projects with established cavers. Remember, the hesitation they may initially show is not personal, but a way to help protect the caves and keep untrained and ill-equipped people from hurting themselves.

CAVING GEAR: A QUICK OVERVIEW

Caving is one of the few outdoor adventure activities that does not require hundreds of dollars of equipment to get started. You can get most of the gear from your local outdoor store, supercenter, or army-surplus store.

BASIC CAVING GEAR

Rugged clothing.	Three sources of light.	Food.
Knee and elbow pads.	Quality helmet.	Water.
Boots.	Spare batteries and lightbulbs.	Cave pack.

CLOTHING

The type of clothes that you wear underground is dependent on the cave temperature, how wet it is, the type of cave, your own comfort level, and, of course, your budget. If you are just starting out and aren't sure if caving is right for you, the best option is to grab some old worn clothes and wear them over something that will keep you warm. In general, cotton is a bad idea: When it's wet, it won't keep you warm. But since most of us have a couple of old pairs of jeans and T-shirts lying around, these will do for your outer layer. Dress in layers. If you are moving quickly, you will need less clothing than when you slow down or stop. You may prefer coveralls, especially in muddy caves where mud and sand can get inside your clothes. These can range from thin mechanic-style cover-alls to custom-designed nylon or PVC models.

A PVC suit can be used for wet caving.
PHOTO BY CARLETON BERN

Underneath your outer clothes, wear something that will keep you warm even when wet, such as wool long johns or a medium-weight material like Capilene that will wick moisture away from your skin but not cause evaporative cooling. It's easy to pack a wicking balaclava in a resealable plastic bag on the inside of your helmet for emergencies. After your first couple of trips, you'll figure out what works best for you.

When you plan a caving trip, the most important thing to consider is the type of cave you will be exploring. The type of equipment and clothing you need will be dictated by the character and environment of the cave. Below, I've broken down some of the general types of caves and the common dress for each.

For Average Caves

Average caves are the most common type throughout the East, the Midwest, and the lower elevations of the Rockies. These caves are damp with small streams and dripping water; temperatures are usually in the fifties. Most cavers wear jeans or heavy nylon pants with a wicking synthetic shirt, or nylon caving coveralls, depending on how wet the cave is or how long the trip is going to be. Underneath, most wear light or mid-weight Capilene tops and bottoms, and most have at least a spare, dry Capilene top in their packs.

If exploring the cave involves sections of swimming or long periods of wading, you will need to wear nylon caving coveralls or thin wet suits. Do not wear cotton clothes in a wet cave. Many cavers wear medium-weight Capilene tops under both wet suit and coveralls, and wear Capilene or wool bottoms inside the nylon coveralls. You should

TABLE 2-1: CAVING CLOTHING BY CAVE TYPE

	Average Cave	Dry Desert Cave	Wet Cave	Cold Damp Cave	Dry Alpine Cave	Wet Alpine Cave
Temperature F	50s	60–70s	50s	40s	30s	30s
Typical Caving	some small streams or pools to cross, lots of dripping water	no rivers or streams, but high humidity	swimming or long sections of wading required	dripping water with some wet walls, but few to no pools or streams	dripping water with some wet walls, but few to no pools or streams	stream crawls, pools, and constant dripping
Outerwear	jeans or caving coveralls, long-sleeved shirt	jeans or shorts, T-shirt	caving coveralls, PVC suit, or thin wet suit	jeans or PVC or nylon caving pants, long-sleeved shirt	jeans or PVC or nylon caving pants, long-sleeved shirt	nylon caving suit or wet suit
Underwear (Tops and Bottoms)	lightweight Capilene	normal	medium-weight Capilene or wool	medium-weight Capilene	medium-weight Capilene	heavyweight Capilene, fleece suit, or equivalent
Typical Extra Clothing Packed	light- to medium-weight Capilene shirt	none	medium-weight Capilene shirt, balaclava	balaclava	balaclava, wool or Capilene glove liners	heavier-weight balaclava, warm glove liners, sometimes extra Capilene kept dry for emergencies

keep a dry Capilene top and balaclava packed so they will stay dry even if you get your pack wet.

For Warm Desert Caves

These caves are typical in the Southwest, particularly West Texas, Arizona, and the Guadalupe Mountains of New Mexico. Typically the caves are dry except for some active dripping or pool areas, and they're around sixty to seventy degrees. Most cavers wear jeans or sometimes nylon shorts with a thin, wicking shirt. Cotton shirts tend to absorb sweat (and if you're moving at all, you're sweating) and will smell bad on even a short trip. Unless you are going to be on a long survey or photo trip, it is unlikely that you will need to pack additional warm clothes, but a lightweight, long-sleeved Capilene top won't hurt.

For High-Elevation Caves

Typical of the Rockies and other mountainous areas, high-elevation caves generally feature temperatures in the forties and are characterized by dripping areas and damp walls and floors. Some cavers still wear cotton jeans, but unless you know your personal limitations and warmth requirements, I advise against it. Nylon or PVC caving suits or caving pants over midweight Capilene will provide better protection against the cold. Carry a spare Capilene top and balaclava in case you need them.

If the cave involves long sections of wading or swimming, you will need a wet or dry suit. Dry suits tend to be more prone to damage and will not function if water gets into them, so it's best to wear nylon coveralls over them. If you are going to spend any time with your upper body out of the water, wear a midweight Capilene top underneath your wet suit. For emergencies, carry a spare Capilene top and balaclava.

For Alpine Caves

Novice cavers should not go into alpine caves, which are found above 10,000 feet or at lower altitudes in northern latitudes. They generally have temperatures in the thirties. In this type of cave, cotton is a killer. Wear caving coveralls or caving pants, medium-weight Capilene underwear, and most likely some kind of polypropylene or wool glove liners. You will also need a spare, dry midweight Capilene top and balaclava in your pack.

If you'll be wading, crawling, or swimming in an alpine cave, you will need more specialized clothing. I recommend a nylon or PVC suit with a thick fleece suit or expedition-weight Capilene underneath. You need a medium- or expedition-weight balaclava and warm glove liners inside more water-resistant gloves, since soaked leather or canvas gloves will quickly numb your hands. Never go into this type of cave without spare dry, warm clothes, for both top and bottom.

OTHER EQUIPMENT

You need more than the right clothing to explore a cave. You also need good boots, gloves, knee and elbow pads, a helmet, and lights. The following sections will tell you what to look for.

Boots

For additional protection, wear sturdy hiking boots, not tennis shoes. Tennis shoes, even high-topped basketball shoes, provide very little ankle support or protection against shifting rocks. Boots with softer soles (usually made with blond-colored rubber) generally stick to the floors better than the hard, black-soled boots. Some cavers prefer high-topped rubber boots, especially for slippery, wet caves. If you are going to a wet

Nonmarking caving boots: leather work boot (left), leather and nylon cross-trainer (right). PHOTOS BY PAUL BURGER

cave, wool or synthetic-blend hiking socks will keep your feet warmer than cotton. For long sections of wading or swimming, you may consider investing in a pair of lightweight neoprene socks; they will keep you relatively warm and won't abrade your feet as much as wool or synthetic-blend socks.

Gloves

Wear gloves to protect your hands while crawling and climbing, or if you're going to be doing any work with ropes. I recommend gloves with leather that covers at least your palm, if not your whole hand. If you are going to be spending a great deal of time in water crawling or swimming, most cavers prefer some kind of sturdy rubber glove. Gloves made mostly of cotton will wear out quickly and tend to deteriorate with repeated soakings.

Knee Pads

If the caves you are exploring require any kind of crawling—and let's face it, most of them do—wear a good pair of knee pads. Most athletic knee pads work fine, and it's up to you whether to wear them under or over your outerwear. Some cavers like the in-line-skating-style hard plastic knee pads, although they have slick surfaces that make it difficult to crawl up a steep mud slope or get a grip on solid rock.

There are pads that cover only the front of the knee, while others surround the entire knee. The regular, knee-only pads are easy to find and comfortable, but tend to slip some while you're crawling. They also do not provide much protection to the side of the knees. The wraparound knee pads are generally made of neoprene and protect the knee and sides of the knee very well. These pads tend to stay in place, but they can rub the back of your knee and may also get very warm. The type you choose will depend on what kind of cave you are in and how much crawling you will be doing. It's probably best to start with regular athletic knee pads and move to the wraparound type if you find you need additional protection.

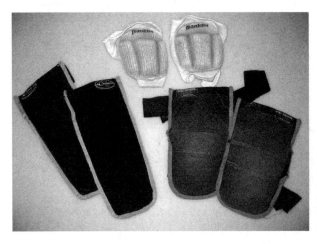

Typical knee pads: long caving pads (left), athletic pads (top), short caving pads (right).
PHOTO BY PAUL BURGER

Many cavers, particularly those who have been caving a long time and already have joint problems, also wear elbow pads. Elbow pads also come in the elbow-only style and wraparound style, with the same benefits and disadvantages as their knee-pad counterparts.

Contacts or Glasses

If you happen to be one of the unfortunate folks who have to wear contacts or glasses all the time, you will have to decide which to wear underground. Glasses are easily broken or scratched, and—worst of all—they can fog up when you're moving. If you opt to wear glasses, use some kind of strap to keep them from falling, and apply defogging treatment to the lenses.

Contact lenses are not the ultimate solution, however. Most caves are dirty, and even the smallest bit of grit behind your contact lens can be excruciating, especially with hard contacts. To make matters worse, it is very difficult to get your hands clean to deal with contact lenses. If you wear contacts caving, make sure you have a couple of disposable sanitary wipes for your hands and a small amount of cleaning solution. If you normally use hard lenses, consider wearing disposable soft contacts and carrying an extra pair in your pack or bringing a pair of glasses in a hard case.

Helmets

As you will most likely discover on your first caving trip, a good helmet is one of the most important pieces of equipment you own. It doesn't matter how long you've been caving, you *will* either bump your head or have something fall on it. Use a sturdy helmet with a reliable chin strap. The chin strap is necessary to keep the helmet on your head if you fall and when you are climbing. Also, make sure the chin strap has a quick-release buckle. Helmets with normal woven-type buckles are virtually impossible to release under a load. There have been several caving accidents in which a caver has dropped down a tight space and gotten caught by the helmet. In a few instances, this has led to serious neck injury and even strangulation.

Climbing helmets work best and are the most widely available, but you will probably have to replace the standard buckle with a quick-release model. Use a climbing helmet approved by the UIAA (Union International des Associations d'Alpinisme)

Typical caving helmets with different ventilation and suspension systems. PHOTO BY PAUL BURGER

with a four-point suspension like those found at most outdoor stores. A construction hard hat with a chin strap is a reasonable substitute for a climbing helmet on your first couple of trips, but not for serious caving. Head protection such as bicycle helmets, baseball or football helmets, and motorcycle helmets are not good for caving and will mark you instantly as a novice to any cavers you meet underground.

LIGHTS

First, and most important, use a headlamp for caving. A handheld flashlight occupies one of your hands and is easily dropped. Though there are few things more amusing than watching a novice try to climb with a flashlight in her mouth, this is *not* the way to go. It's best to have at least three independent sources of light, meaning that each should be able to operate without relying on power or parts from another light. Your primary light and at least one of your backups should be a headlamp. Many cavers will have a small handheld penlight such as a Mini Maglite or LED Photon as a third source of light. These can be worn on a lanyard around your neck for easy access.

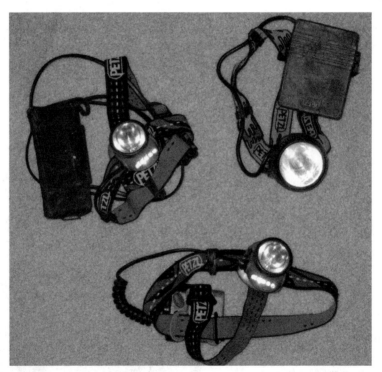

Typical caving lights (clockwise from upper left): LED with belt-mounted battery pack (four C-sized), incandescent with helmet-mounted battery pack (three C-sized), and LED with helmet-mounted battery pack (four AA-sized). PHOTO BY PAUL BURGER

There are two basic lighting systems you can choose from, carbide and electric. Much like the debate between Mac and PC users, each type has its vocal supporters. Carbide is generally cheaper to operate, gives off heat that can be used to keep warm, and gives a soft, warm light. On the other hand, carbide lights are messier than electric and require constant maintenance. Electric lights are more expensive to operate and generate more waste; some cavers dislike the more harsh light and rings of light projected by lightbulbs. They are, however, less finicky and more water-resistant than carbide, and with improvements in bulb and battery technology, they are almost as cheap as carbide lights to operate.

Electric Lights

There are two basic types of electric headlamps out there: those that run on the standard incandescent bulbs, including krypton and halogen bulbs, and lights that use light-emitting diodes (LEDs). One thing common to all the systems is that the brighter the light, the more battery power it will take to run it, and the more batteries you will have to buy and carry.

Besides the basic choice of incandescent versus LED, you need to decide if you want your battery pack mounted on your head or on your belt. If you have the batteries on your helmet, there will be more weight—which could result in a sore neck, particularly if you're doing a lot of crawling or are hunched over a sketchbook while surveying. Wearing your batteries on your belt, on the other hand, means contending with a cord. It's very easy to get your battery cord snagged on floor and wall protrusions. Some cavers remedy this problem by running their cord through their shirts or inside their coveralls, but this can be a pain if you have to take off your battery pack to fit through a tight passage.

As with most equipment, the choice of light type and battery is a matter of personal preference and not one of safety. The best advice is to try out a number of different types to see what works best for you and the type of caving you're doing. Look at what most cavers in your area are using to gauge what is best.

COMMON CHARACTERISTICS OF A GOOD CAVING LIGHT

- Enough power to last through your typical cave trip without a large number of extra batteries.
- Easy-to-purchase batteries. Some headlamps require special batteries that are not readily available.
- Solid, shock-resistant parts.
- A water-resistant headpiece and battery pack.
- A sturdy, thick cord and solid connections at the headpiece and battery pack.
- A reliable way to mount the light on your helmet. You don't want to have to tape your headlamp to your helmet.

Incandescent Lights

When you buy a generic headlamp from your local superstore or sporting goods store, it usually comes standard with an incandescent bulb with a specific type of gas inside—krypton, halogen, or something similar. Depending on the type of bulb and battery combination, you can get widely different results.

FACTORS AFFECTING YOUR LAMP LIFE

- Battery type (alkaline versus lithium, and so on—see the discussion under "Battery Types").
- Battery power output.
- Bulb brightness.
- Power regulation. Most new headlamps have chips that regulate power use to maximize light efficiency.
- Cave temperature. Most lights run less efficiently at low temperatures, so you will go through batteries more quickly in a cold cave.

To determine how much life you will get out of a headlamp, refer to the manufacturer's technical data, which can be found on the packages. Keep in mind that most manufacturers give very optimistic numbers, and the lamp will not perform as well under real caving conditions.

All types of incandescent bulbs will burn out after being used, so make sure you have at least a couple of spares in your cave pack. Many headlamps have spaces for an extra bulb on the headpiece, but it's a good idea to have backups in your pack as well. Remember that rough handling (and almost any type of caving would be considered rough handling) can break the filament in your backup bulbs, so be sure to pack them well. You can easily pack extra bulbs in film canisters along with tissue or cotton balls.

LEDs

The price of high-intensity LEDs has recently dropped, and the technology keeps improving so there are now affordable LED headlamps. With the correct circuitry, you can get much more life out of an LED than a regular bulb. This is especially important if you are going to be taking very long cave trips and/or hauling gear very deep into a cave. The longer the battery life, the fewer batteries you have to carry, and the lighter your pack will be.

Most of the widely available LED headlamps are not as bright as their incandescent counterparts, but the light is generally more than enough to navigate through a cave. Another disadvantage is the inability to focus an LED light, making it difficult to produce a spotlight to look at holes in the ceiling or observe distant objects. Many cavers who use LED lights as their primary light source will keep a small flashlight solely for spotting. Some of the newer one-watt LEDs are focusable.

The light from LEDs looks bluish compared with standard bulbs or carbide, but is actually much closer to sunlight. After you use them for a while, you hardly notice the difference unless you are caving with people using regular bulbs. LED lights produce an even glow like carbide lamps and do not have the bright rings often associated with electric lights.

Good LED lights can be regulated and have multiple settings so that you can selectively use less or more light at the flick of a switch. You may want more light for viewing a large room than you need for traveling; you may want less while you're sitting eating lunch. When you dim an LED, it maintains the same color and does not become orange like an incandescent bulb. The ability to dim the LED increases the efficiency of the headlamp and will let you get much more life out of a set of batteries.

Battery Types

In addition to different types of bulbs, there are a wide variety of batteries that can be used for caving. The most widely available and most commonly used are alkaline. Buy a good brand and avoid the off-brand bulk batteries. Even though they are technically the same, experience has shown that off-brands do not last as long and have worse quality control. Unfortunately, name-brand batteries can be expensive, more than a dollar each, and that can add up to a lot of money over a caving career.

Lithium-ion batteries are rechargeable and significantly more expensive than alkaline and NiCad batteries, but they are much lighter. You will also have problems finding replacement batteries at most stores. Lithium batteries last much longer than alkaline batteries but are not rechargeable. They are lightweight but very expensive. They are, however, the most efficient battery under cold conditions.

Another option is rechargeable batteries. Nickel-cadmium (NiCad) batteries and rechargers can be bought at many electronics stores, but are generally much more expensive than alkaline. The ability to recharge the batteries results in a long-term savings over alkaline. However, a NiCad battery is heavier and holds less charge than an alkaline.

Nickel-metal-hydride (NiMH) batteries are now becoming more widely available and are slowly replacing the alkaline battery for many cavers. These batteries are much cheaper than lithium, can be recharged, provide roughly the same amount of life, and weigh about the same as an alkaline battery.

Your best bet is either alkaline batteries or rechargeable nickel-metal-hydride. These are the cheapest, most widely available battery types and will provide you enough light for a typical cave trip.

Carbide Lights

Carbide lights use calcium carbide in a chamber to which water can slowly be added. The reaction between carbide and water produces acetylene, which is then burned to make light. During the course of a long caving trip, you will probably have to change

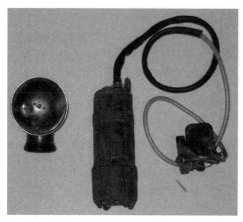

Two types of carbide lamp: cap lamp (left), belt-mounted "ceiling burner" (right).

PHOTO BY PAUL BURGER

carbide at least once and will need a container to keep the spent carbide from getting all over your pack or the cave.

The most common type of carbide light in the United States is the *brass cap lamp*, which many people have seen on the helmets of miners in old photos. Cap lamps require a special bracket mounted to your helmet. You put carbide into the base of the container and screw the top on. You then fill the top reservoir with water and adjust the lamp until the water is dripping at about one drip per second. Place your palm across the face of the reflector with the heel of your hand on the striking wheel. Your hand should trap a small amount of gas, and as you slide your hand down across the striker, the gas should ignite with a nice pop. One charge of carbide should give you two to five hours of good light, depending on how much carbide the lamp carries and how large a flame you burn. Since cleaning the base out between charges takes time and has the potential to drop spent carbide into the cave, many cavers bring an extra base full of carbide and fitted with a good lid. Then you only have to swap bases to keep going for another four or so hours.

What do you do if the lamp doesn't light or isn't giving you a good flame? This could mean that the striker didn't light the gas, the lamp isn't generating gas, or the gas isn't getting out of the reservoir. Here are some basic steps to troubleshoot the problem:

1. Stick your tongue in front of the tip to feel if there is gas coming out. If so, try striking the wheel again, or use someone else's flame or a lighter to ignite the gas.

2. Use the tip cleaner from your carbide kit to clean out the tip, then repeat step 1.

3. Open the lamp to see if there is water dripping. If you do not see about a drop per second, adjust the lever to increase the flow. Once the water starts, reassemble the lamp and go to step 1.

4. If water is still not coming out, put your mouth over the reservoir opening and suck air backward through the drip tube. This will clear any small amounts of grit that may be clogging the drip tube. If the dripping starts, go to step 1. If you still cannot get water to drip after these measures, there must be something seriously wrong with the lamp—or it may be very dirty—and you will probably have to use your backup light for the rest of the trip. You should thoroughly clean your lamp once you get back home.

5. If your drip is fine and the tip is clear, but you still do not feel the gas coming through, then check the "felt" filter in the base of the unit. If the felt gets wet (from setting the drip too high to begin with) or gets too dirty, it will not allow the gas to come through. Replace it with the spare from your repair kit and try again.

It's very important to clean your lamp as soon as possible after the trip. If you leave spent carbide in the lamp, it will corrode the metal and turn hard as a rock, making the lamp very difficult to clean. As most carbide cavers will tell you, there is nothing more annoying than having to chisel weeks-old carbide out of the bottom of a lamp.

Never dump spent carbide inside the cave or on the ground when you get out. Carbide has a fairly salty taste that is attractive to some animals—but it's toxic and can kill even large animals such as cows, horses, and deer.

Another kind of carbide light in common use is the *carbide generator* or ceiling burner, as it's more commonly referred to in the United States. This light uses carbide in a large canister worn on the hip with a long tube that goes up to your helmet. You should get six to eight hours of light out of one charge of carbide. As the nickname suggests, the flame on this type of light is much larger and gives off more light than a standard cap lamp. The light can be difficult to use in crawlways since it goes out if the generator is turned on its side, but most are equipped with a piezoelectric lighter that allows you to light the gas with a flick of your wrist. This light is very popular in Europe and for U.S. cavers working in places like Mexico. Since it's hard to find at most outdoor stores and caving equipment vendors, I will not go into serious detail on troubleshooting these lamps, though the concepts are the same as the cap lamp.

One final point on carbide lamps: Due to increasing security concerns, it's getting more and more difficult to ship carbide. This can make it hard to obtain in some areas. Make sure you have a good, reliable source of carbide before investing in a carbide lamp.

ITEMS FOR A CARBIDE REPAIR KIT

- Tip cleaner.
- Spare felt.
- Spare tip.
- Spare gasket.
- Small screwdriver or penknife to scrape carbide out of the base.
- Small lighter.
- Spare base (optional).

SUGGESTED ADDITIONAL GEAR

- Trash bag for dirty clothes after the trip.
- Clean change of clothes, including shoes.
- Water for after the trip.
- Post-trip snack food.
- Bandanna or hat to disguise "helmet hair."
- Solar shower for cleaning up after caving, or a good supply of wet towelettes (especially when you are caving for multiple days).

BASIC SAFETY

While many types of accidents are common to any type of caving, some basic guidelines can keep you out of trouble.

With these guidelines and the advice given on specific types of caves in later chapters, you should be prepared to start your caving adventures.

LOW-IMPACT CAVING

It's important to protect not only yourself while exploring caves, but also the cave and cave environment. Unlike the surface where worn trails can grow over and geological processes are constantly reshaping the land, caves recover slowly from impacts, if at all. Low-impact caving is the best way to keep a cave looking the way you first saw it for those who come after you.

There are many simple things you can do to keep caves protected. The basic guidelines are: "Leave nothing but footprints, take nothing but pictures, and kill nothing but time."

Leave Nothing but Footprints

First, pack out everything you pack in. Candy wrappers, batteries, and spent carbide are obvious forms of litter you should not leave in a cave. Heavily visited caves often feature cave walls painted or smoked with arrows, names, and other graffiti. These marks are almost impossible to get off the walls. If you wish to make a record of your visit, do so in a caving journal, not in the cave.

Human waste can be a large problem in some caves, especially those not prone to seasonal flooding. This type of waste is disgusting for later visitors and adds a foreign nutrient source into the delicate cave ecosystem. Even though it deteriorates rapidly on the surface, human waste can remain for years in the underground environment. Sturdy plastic bottles can be used to remove liquid wastes. It's easier for women to use a wide-mouthed bottle or a specialized funnel (available at outdoor stores) for bottles with smaller openings. Solid waste can be collected in multiple layers of resealable plastic bags. I strongly suggest using a layer of aluminum foil as a vapor barrier: The plastic will breathe and let the smell out. You and the rest of your team will be glad you added foil.

Other types of litter are less obvious but still can have a negative impact on the cave environment. Smoke of any kind contaminates cave walls with not only soot, but also other chemicals that can kill cave life and damage walls and decorations. Crumbs are a major source of foreign nutrients into the cave system. Most popular caves contain a favorite spot where you can almost always find spots of mold and fungus growing on dropped food crumbs. When you eat, do it over an open plastic bag to collect crumbs. Eating over your open pack will cover your gear with crumbs that will drop when you take something out of it.

A taped trail limits impact to a narrow path through a delicate cave passage. PHOTO BY PAUL BURGER

Although the basic guideline is to leave nothing but footprints, even this must be done carefully. Black-soled boots can leave black marks on rock floors and flowstone. If you aren't sure whether your boots leave marks, drag them across a piece of concrete. If they mark the cement, they will mark the cave. You should be able to find light-colored soles that work just as well without marking the cave.

Every step you take has an impact, whether you are walking across a delicate floor or an area that appears to have been pounded by a million other visitors. If the cave you are exploring has flagged or taped trails, stay between the markers. If it doesn't, choose the path that already has the most impact.

Take Nothing but Pictures

The best souvenir of your caving trip is a nice collection of photos (and some nice bruises and scrapes to show to your friends). Do not remove anything else from a cave. Speleothems take hundreds or thousands of years to grow. Out of the cave, a formation will lose its luster and eventually look like just another rock. Even if you do not break the formation, touching it can leave behind oils, dirt, and mud from your hands and cause it to stop growing.

Do not remove historical artifacts or archaeological or paleontological materials from a cave. To understand these things and their importance, they must be studied in context. Observe them, appreciate them, and leave them for others to enjoy and study. If you are on a cave trip involving trash cleanup and aren't sure whether something is historic, leave it and let the experts make the call. In most federal- and state-managed caves, there are laws and strict penalties for disturbing these types of objects. Many states also have laws to help protect privately owned caves.

Kill Nothing but Time

Almost every cave contains some type of life. Snakes, spiders, and many insects are just temporary residents that like the cool entrance zones. Bats, cave crickets, salamanders, and crayfish are more permanent residents. No matter what cave critter you encounter, remember that you are the visitor. Most cave residents have no interest in you; they will leave you alone if you leave them alone.

This rule also applies to microbial life. Try not to add foreign materials into the ecosystem or destroy habitat. This means you should not drop crumbs in the cave, leave your waste, or contaminate pools by walking through them, especially in caves that do not flood periodically.

Practicing these low-impact caving techniques will help protect the cave so that it can be enjoyed by others. They can also help you to be more observant of your surroundings while underground. Observation is the key to most caving, allowing you to navigate to avoid potentially dangerous situations, and to protect the cave environment.

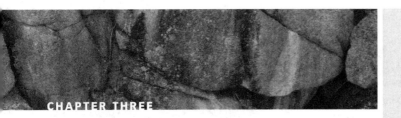

CHAPTER THREE

Horizontal Caving

ADDITIONAL
EQUIPMENT

ORIENTEERING—
CAVE MAPS

TECHNIQUES

Now that you have caving clothes, a good helmet, and a reliable light, you're ready to start some serious exploration—*almost*. First you'll need a few more pieces of gear and a working knowledge of cave maps and caving techniques.

ADDITIONAL EQUIPMENT

Before you step into a cave, you'll want a good pack, food and water, and some emergency supplies.

Cave Pack

As a caver, your best friend or worst enemy can be your cave pack. A bulky pack will snag on cave walls and make crawlways more difficult, while a small one won't hold everything you need for your trip. In order to pick the best pack size, spread all of your gear on the floor and see what kind of volume you will need. Remember, for longer trips, you may need to allow extra room to bring out trash and human waste.

At first you can probably get away with a small day pack, but these usually have too many straps and do not hold up to the wear and tear of caving for more than a couple of trips. Side packs generally work better because they're smaller, but it's difficult to find true side packs at most outdoor shops. A military-surplus gas mask bag is a good solution. These packs hold up well under pretty rugged caving and generally cost less than $10. Make sure you get one with the waist strap intact. If you use the strap, the pack will not drag on the ground and will last longer. You will need to add something to keep the pack closed securely so nothing can fall out. The cheapest and most effective solution is to cut a section of old inner tube across its diameter to create a large rubber band. This simple loop is very effective at keeping your pack tightly closed.

You can buy a fanny pack at most outdoor shops. Choose one with a minimum number of straps and loops. These will only snag and hold you up while you are trying to move through the cave. Find one with the lowest profile you can. Remember, you're likely to be crawling at some point, and you don't want a fat pack to get in the way. Many cavers who use fanny packs will slide them around to the front for crawlways and remove them for tight passages.

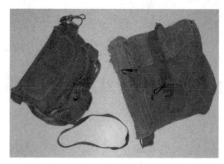

At left is an army-surplus gas mask bag with an inner tube "rubber band" to keep the contents secure. On the right is an army surplus rucksack. PHOTO BY PAUL BURGER

If you need more capacity for longer or gear-intensive trips (such as vertical caves or photo trips), most caving suppliers have solid, nylon packs designed specifically for caving. Caving equipment vendors carry several sizes of side packs, usually made of tough, cave-tested nylon or PVC. Some of these can be worn either on your back or as side packs, though they tend to work much better as backpacks.

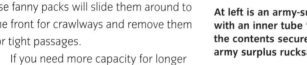

Cave packs are usually made of tough nylon or PVC. Nylon resists abrasion better, but the fabric will hold dirt and mud, which can spread to cleaner parts of a cave. PVC packs are more water-resistant, are easy to clean even during a cave trip, and slide across the ground more easily than nylon packs, but they wear out faster, too. At most outdoor stores you will only find nylon packs.

Typical medium to large PVC cave packs.
PHOTO BY PAUL BURGER

Food

Food is mostly a matter of personal preference; cavers figure out their favorites after only a few trips. No matter how well you think you have packed your food, it will get bumped, smashed, and shaken. You do not want to bring easily bruised foods like bananas and apples unless you enjoy sucking banana mush out of your spare shirt when you get hungry. You also want to avoid drinks like soda that could potentially explode in your pack. There is nothing more disconcerting than hearing that telltale hiss coming from the bottom of your pack.

To protect the cave, avoid crumbly foods that could spill. Many of the energy bars available at grocery stores tend to be soft and do not generate crumbs. If you carry a sandwich, put it inside a resealable plastic container or, at the very least, a heavy-duty, resealable sandwich bag. This will keep your sandwich from squishing all over your pack and keep dirt, grit, spent carbide, and other things out of your food.

Some cavers like small cans of food such as tuna, sausages, and fruit. It's very hard to get all of the juice out of the cans; package the empties so they do not leak into your pack. Also, do not smash the can flat in the cave; this can cause undue damage to the cave floor and increases the possibility of leaving behind food particles.

WHAT TO EAT—WHAT *NOT* TO EAT

Typical Caver Cuisine	Foods to Avoid
Energy bars.	Fresh fruit.
Jerky.	Soda pop.
Sandwiches on bagels.	Dry granola bars (crumbs).
Hard candies.	Sandwiches on regular bread.
Trail mix or dried fruit.	
Small cans of fruit or meats.	

You'll also want to carry some water in a container that will hold up to the rigors of caving. Used soda pop bottles work well, but they wear out faster than the tough, screw-top plastic bottles made for hiking. For most trips a liter of water should work, depending on how fast you are moving, how difficult the trip is, how warm the cave is, and how long you are going to be underground.

Emergency Equipment

While it's impossible to pack for every contingency, there are some basic things every caver should carry for medical emergencies and equipment failures. Which ones you need depends on the type of gear you have, the cave trip itself, your training, and your experience. Do make sure you have backup bulbs for every light you are carrying, not just for your primary light. Carry enough batteries to last at least two or three times the length of the trip. This will ensure you have enough light, even if something goes terribly wrong.

Many cavers like to bring a small, basic first-aid kit along with some over-the-counter painkillers and anti-inflammatories (such as aspirin and ibuprofen). You may also want to carry small amounts of antacid and antidiarrhea medicine. A film canister makes a good catchall waterproof pill container. For longer or more serious trips, consider bringing an elastic bandage and some moleskin to handle minor twists and blisters. If you have the space, a flexible metal SAM Splint can be very handy, especially for more serious ankle and wrist injuries. A less obvious, but very important, item for your first-aid kit is a small pad of paper and a pencil. During an emergency, you may need to write down basic information about the injured, including vital signs, age, type of accident, and any other information you can gather to give to medical personnel.

You do not need to bring a large first-aid kit into a cave. There is little in a kit to treat serious injuries, and adhesive bandages are not likely to stay on a cut through a cave trip. Also, regardless of what type of first-aid kit you bring along, check it frequently to make sure that medicines have not expired and all the sterile packaging is still intact. Otherwise, all you are doing is carrying extra weight.

Even if you never need a first-aid kit, you will at some point need to make repairs to your equipment. A sewing awl with thread can be used to make quick, strong repairs to pack straps, clothes, and other caving gear and is especially useful on longer cave trips. They are easy to use, but you should practice on the surface so you don't have to learn underground under difficult conditions.

One item that you will find in nearly every caver's pack is a small roll of duct tape. This can be used to fix battery packs, hold lights to a helmet, and perform an almost infinite number of other minor repairs. Duct tape can be used to help secure bandages and splints as well as aid in many other first-aid procedures. Do not use tape to patch holes in your clothes or knee pads; the tape will only fall off into the cave as trash. The best way to carry tape is to wrap 3 to 6 feet around the outside of your water bottle. It takes up very little space this way and holds up even on wet trips.

Forty feet of 1-inch, tubular webbing is a great thing to have along. If you encounter a climb or pit that is too difficult for easy free climbing, you can quickly rig this as a handline. A supply of webbing can also come in handy when making emergency repairs to cave packs and other equipment, especially if you have a sewing awl.

You will probably need a few more emergency supplies if you are going to be in a very cold cave. In this type of cave, spare dry clothes are a must. If you have the space, consider packing a small alcohol stove. These stoves are self-contained inside a small pot that can be used to boil water. Small heat tab stoves can be used to warm small amounts of water and cans of soup. The fumes from heat tab stoves can be poisonous, so do not use them in small or poorly ventilated areas. You can also bring heat packs in case of an emergency, but make sure they are well packaged so they do not activate prematurely.

Simple alcohol stove and pot (pencil for scale). PHOTO BY PAUL BURGER

With these few items, you should be able to handle most minor emergencies and equipment problems. As you gain experience with caving and your equipment, you will probably discover more essentials.

ORIENTEERING—CAVE MAPS

Good cave maps are becoming much easier to find, especially if you are exploring with an organized caving group. All maps will have a plan view that shows what the cave would look like if the roof were removed. Some also include a profile that shows what the cave would look like from the side if you could see through the rock, and sometimes cross sections to give you an idea of the passage shape.

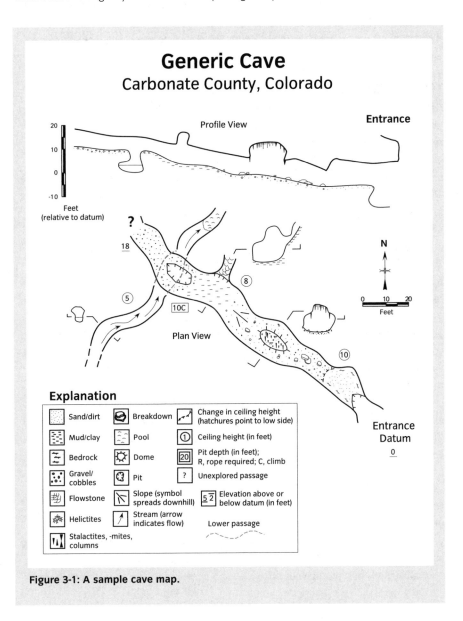

Generic Cave
Carbonate County, Colorado

Profile View

Entrance

20
10
0
-10

Feet
(relative to datum)

?

18

5

8

10C

Plan View

10

N

0   10   20
Feet

Explanation

Sand/dirt	Breakdown	Change in ceiling height (hatchures point to low side)	
Mud/clay	Pool	Ceiling height (in feet)	
Bedrock	Dome	Pit depth (in feet); R, rope required; C, climb	
Gravel/ cobbles	Pit	? Unexplored passage	
Flowstone	Slope (symbol spreads downhill)	5 2 Elevation above or below datum (in feet)	
Helictites	Stream (arrow indicates flow)	Lower passage	
Stalactites, -mites, columns			

Entrance Datum

0

Figure 3-1: A sample cave map.

Most maps have a north arrow, but you need to make sure it indicates true north and not magnetic north. If the cave is oriented to true north, readings you take with your compass may be up to eighteen degrees different from the map, depending on what part of the country you are in. This difference between true north and magnetic north is called *declination*. You should be able to get your local declination from any regular topographic map that covers the area where you are caving.

Cave maps use a special set of symbols to indicate drops and climbs, the materials that cover the floor, and cave decorations. A good map will have a key explaining what these symbols mean, but just in case, figure 3-1 includes some of the most common symbols along with a sample cave map.

TECHNIQUES

Caving is a combination of hiking, climbing, and crawling through an obstacle course of pits, boulders, water, tiny holes and cracks in solid rock, and other obstructions. As a result, moving through a cave efficiently and safely is an art.

The best way to explore a cave without damaging it—or yourself—is to move smoothly. Most beginning cavers, especially men, try to overcome their lack of experience with brute force. You do not want to fight the cave; the cave will win every time. It takes awhile to develop your cave legs and learn how to move your body through this alien environment.

If you are stumbling a lot and having to use the walls and ceiling to keep your balance, you are moving too quickly. Slow down to a pace at which you still have to work, but without constantly using the cave for balance. As you gain confidence and learn to move through caves, you will find you are moving faster.

If you do have to use the walls for balance, put your hands where others have already touched. Try using just your fingers instead of your whole hand to minimize your impact. Your palms tend to get more dirty than the back of your hand, so maintain your balance with your fist instead. If your gloves are very dirty, you may have to take them off to move through some passages.

Always look ahead to anticipate how you are going to move your body through the next section of passage or how you are going to get past the next obstacle. You would think that consciously thinking about the next several moves would slow you down, but it eventually becomes habit and helps you move through the cave more smoothly.

Almost every caver has been snagged while going through a small or narrow passage. There are two ways you can deal with this problem: You can yank yourself free, or you can stop, free the snag, and keep going. Even though it seems like yanking yourself free is the faster option, you will be expending much more energy. Also, if your tear your clothes, you will have less protection, and the tear will be more prone to snagging later. It's best to stop, back up or step back down, free the snag, and then continue. The same applies to getting your boot stuck. You can almost always free your foot by backing up or reversing your last move and kicking your heel up. If you keep moving, you increase the chances of twisting or breaking your ankle.

Move through the cave headfirst so you can see what is coming up and adjust. Obviously, you do not want to crawl down a pit headfirst; turn around and go feetfirst. If you come upon a steep, downward-sloping crawl and don't know whether it gets steeper or levels out, go feetfirst to be safe. It is very difficult to push yourself back uphill using only your arms. As you learn the characteristics of each cave, you will figure out which obstacles are better negotiated feetfirst and which headfirst.

Never jump in a cave. Jumping down short drops or across gaps can be very dangerous: You don't know how slippery the floor is or if the rock you are jumping onto is stable. It's also difficult to control your balance after a jump, which means it's easy to pitch forward into the wall, into cave decorations, or, worse, down another drop. Even though it may take more time, climb down short drops and carefully step across gaps. A rescue will take much more time and effort than you save by jumping.

Stoopways

A *stoopway* is any section of cave passage that forces you to bend your back to get through. If the stoopway is short, you will probably be able to simply bend over and walk forward while looking down at the ground. This technique does not allow you to look forward, making it difficult to navigate and to see upcoming obstacles. Doing a basic stoop may also cause you to stand up too quickly when the passage begins to open up and make you either bang your helmet or scrape your back on the ceiling.

Stoopwalking to keep beneath delicate cave formations. Note the light-soled caving boots used to keep from marking the flowstone on the floor. PHOTO BY PAUL BURGER

If you need to go long distances or through winding, wide passages, you can do a *sideways stoop*. To do this, shuffle sideways, bent at the waist, with your head turned in the direction you are traveling.

Occasionally switch between leading with your left foot and leading with your right to avoid putting too much stress on only one side of your neck. Very long sections of stoopways will cause pain in your lower back, so you may want to take short breaks every twenty minutes or so, especially if you have a heavy pack swinging from your neck.

In very low stoopways, you can do the sideways stoop with your hands on the floor—a technique sometimes called the *ape walk*. It can be much faster than crawling on your hands and knees if the passage is high enough, and it puts less stress on your lower back than the sideways stoop.

Hands-and-Knees Crawl

Most of us mastered the art of crawling when we were young, but have since forgotten how to do it without causing undue damage to our knees and elbows. The most basic is the hands-and-knees crawl. You don't want to have any type of pack on your back through a crawl. If you only have a backpack, remove it and either push it ahead of you or drag it behind. If you are using a fanny pack, slide it around so it's hanging underneath you.

Bedrock hands-and-knees crawl in a Colorado cave. PHOTO BY PAUL BURGER

Crawling on all fours seems straightforward, but there are a couple of techniques that may make your experience less painful. If the angle of your headlamp is adjustable, pivot it upward so it lights up the passage in front of you instead of the ground right under your head. This makes it easier to see turns and other obstacles so you can adjust your body position before you get to them. If you are wearing good gloves or have strong joints, try using your fists on the ground instead of your palms. Crawling on your palms causes a lot of strain on your wrists and may limit how far you can go. Using your fists puts most of the stress on your arm and shoulder muscles, which can take the pressure better than your wrists.

Belly Crawl

If the passage is very low, you will have to remove your side and fanny packs as well as backpacks. In wide belly crawls, it may be possible to wear a side pack, but make sure the passage does not narrow: It will be difficult to remove your pack once you get going. Push your pack ahead of you or drag it behind you. You should also adjust the angle of your headlamp so it lights the passage ahead and not the ground or wall.

A tight belly crawl squeeze may require exhaling to get through. PHOTO BY PAUL BURGER

The most basic method is the *salamander crawl*. Use your hands to pull yourself forward in a motion similar to climbing a ladder. At the same time use your feet and the sides of your knees to push forward. Unfortunately most knee pads have very little protection on the sides of the knees, so you will have to be careful of rocks or buy pads that completely surround your knees. As you crawl, your hips will move from side to side in the motion that gives the technique its name.

If the crawl is too narrow to allow for the side-to-side motion of the salamander crawl, use a *military crawl*. Instead of having your hands in front of you, cross your arms under your chest so your right fist is at the armpit of your left arm and vice versa. For the military crawl, you will use your elbows instead of your hands to pull yourself forward. Push with your feet just as in the salamander crawl. You won't be able to bend your knees as much in a narrow passage, so you may have to drag your feet behind you and let your elbows do most of the work. You will be very glad to have elbow pads for this type of crawling. You can also use the military crawl to move your pack in a more controlled way. Place your pack across your folded arms and let it travel through the passage there instead of dragging or pushing it. The military crawl is indeed used by the military, and you frequently see pictures of soldiers crawling under barbed wire with their guns across their folded arms. This method is particularly useful if you are carrying something fragile such as photographic equipment.

A variant on the military crawl can be used in higher passages with soft floors. You do the *elbow crawl* by propping up on your elbows and walking on them through the passage while allowing your feet to drag behind you. This can be a fast way to move through certain crawls, but it's very hard on the elbows, even in mud-floored passages; use it only if you have elbow pads.

Squeezes

A squeeze is any passage tighter than a crawl but still large enough for a human. Of course, the more "volumetrically disadvantaged" you are, the more likely it is that small passages will be a squeeze for you. The difficulty of squeezes is based on how large you are, how flexible you are, your pain tolerance, and how well you use the natural shape of your body to fit. There are no techniques that can help you with the first three; to some extent, they can be controlled by diet, exercise, stretching, and practice.

A very tight squeeze in Carlsbad Cavern. PHOTO BY CARLETON BERN

Claustrophobia, the fear of enclosed spaces, is one of the first issues you will have to deal with concerning squeezes. Most cavers were not comfortable in very tight spaces when they first started. It takes time and experience to become comfortable with fitting your body into squeezes. A good way to get experience in tight spaces without going into a cave is to use a *squeeze box*: a wooden tunnel with two open ends and a roof that is adjustable up or down. You'll often find one of these set up at caver parties and gatherings. For cavers, it's like a limbo contest, only much more painful. The adjustable top has quick-release pins to free you if you cannot go any farther. Using a squeeze box will show you what your limits are and help teach you how to move through small spaces. It will also make you more comfortable when you get into a real cave squeeze.

Some tight spots are narrow as well as low. If the passage is narrow and not tall enough for you to simply fit by moving through on your side, you will need to minimize your width. You don't have much control over how wide your hips are, since they are made of bone, but you can control the width of your shoulders: Make yourself narrower by placing one arm ahead of you and one arm behind. This allows you to pull with your forward arm and push with your other one.

For those with broad shoulders, place both arms over your head. Your shoulder muscles rotate into the space between your collarbone and neck. You can't push this way, but you can usually reduce your width by several inches.

Unless you are very skinny, you don't ever want to go through a squeeze with both arms at your side. If you get wedged, both arms will be pinned with no way of gaining leverage; you'll end up needing to be dragged back out by your feet.

If the passage is wide but very low, you can gain some room by exhaling. This will reduce the volume of your chest and allow you to fit through a smaller space. Some squeezes can be negotiated by taking very shallow breaths and moving forward a little bit at a time while exhaling. Be careful using this technique, however: It's possible to exhale and wedge into a space that's too small, which can lead to broken ribs. It's also possible to wedge tight enough to prevent you from being able to inhale again and cause you to suffocate. You should not begin pushing very tight passages until you have been caving for a long time and are very comfortable with your limitations.

In some squeezes you may need to remove your helmet and push it ahead of you to give yourself a bit more space and see what you are doing. If possible, hand your helmet

A two-hand forward crawl. Note that the caver can control his pack with both hands. PHOTO BY PAUL BURGER

to people on the other side of the squeeze and have them light the way so you can focus your efforts on getting through and not pushing gear ahead of you. Keep in mind that your head is now unprotected, and you will have to be much more careful.

Getting Stuck

If you get jammed, do not panic, even if the position you are in is painful. The panic response will cause your body to swell, which can make it even more difficult to get out. Also, if you panic and start flailing around, you will get tired and possibly wedge even more. Close your eyes, take a deep breath, and analyze the situation. Figure out if you are stuck against the rock or if a piece of your clothing or equipment is snagged. Always back out of a squeeze instead of trying to force yourself through. If you try to push through, you run the risk of jamming more tightly. Once you're out it will be easier to figure out a different way to get through. You can strip off some clothes to make it easier, try a different angle, or just decide the passage is too small.

If your clothing or equipment is snagged, see if the person behind you can free the snag. If not, try to free it by moving backward, twisting, and then moving forward again. Hopefully the caver behind you can pull your legs and help you move backward if you cannot get enough leverage on your own. If your pants are snagged, try to undo the snap and zipper and then slide forward out of the pants. You can also have someone help undo your pants to get out of a jam (only if you are on very friendly terms or are very stuck).

Remove your pack if you're not sure you can fit through a small passage with it on; it's much harder to remove your pack once you're already squeezing. If you are going through with your pack on and it snags, try to undo the strap and leave it behind. If that doesn't work, back out and try it without your pack. If you cannot back out, you may need to have the caver behind you pull your legs to help. In some cases the caver in front of you can help pull you through, but you run the risk of getting further trapped.

If you are pressed up against solid rock, it is usually more difficult to get free. Hopefully, you have some leverage to push out of the squeeze with your arms. Otherwise, try backing up with the help of the caver behind you first. It is easier on your body to inch out slowly rather than trying to move quickly. Have the caver behind you pull on your ankles while you wriggle back. After only a few inches, you should be free enough to get out on your own. In a squeeze that you had to exhale to get into, you will need to exhale as the person pulls you back. Make sure to tell your helper when to pull. You don't want the person pulling while you're taking a breath; that's a good way to tear the skin off your chest.

Be careful when squeezing down into a vertical crack. It is always easier to slide down than push yourself back out. When you are going down through a vertical squeeze, think about how you are going to get back out. Will you be able to push off a floor or are you going to depend on your hand- and footholds? Look at the holds that you may use.

If someone gets stuck in a vertical crack and cannot get enough leverage to move, you'll need to assist him. If you're below him, you can squeeze back up into the crack and push his legs, or even provide a shoulder or head to push off. If you're above, you can grab his wrists and try to pull him out. The stuck caver should pull with his arms at the same time. Remember that pulling someone's arms to their full extent can dislocate a shoulder.

If the walls are smooth and the stuck caver cannot push off the floor, consider rigging the crack with an etrier, a simple ladder made of webbing (see figure 7-2 in chapter 7). Rig the etrier to something solid, then lower it past the caver so he can step into one of the loops. With something to push off, a caver can usually free himself.

If this still doesn't work, tie a harness around his legs using webbing or rope. It's best to tie around the stuck caver's legs and hips rather than around his chest to prevent interfering with his breathing or breaking his ribs. The harness will also help to support the caver from slipping farther down even if you cannot get him free.

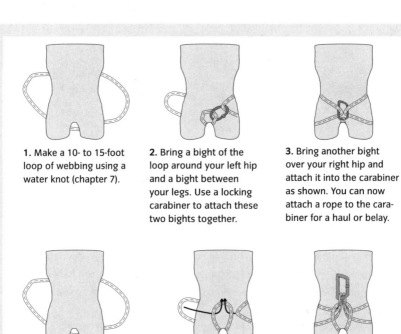

1. Make a 10- to 15-foot loop of webbing using a water knot (chapter 7).

2. Bring a bight of the loop around your left hip and a bight between your legs. Use a locking carabiner to attach these two bights together.

3. Bring another bight over your right hip and attach it into the carabiner as shown. You can now attach a rope to the carabiner for a haul or belay.

You can use a slightly larger loop and attach the carabiner as shown to haul or belay larger people or if you need a higher tie-in point for the carabiner.

Figure 3-2: Using a loop of webbing and a carabiner to construct a makeshift harness.

If you cannot get to his legs and rig a harness, you may have to loop the webbing around his chest underneath his arms. Use several loops of webbing or rope around the chest tied with a bowline on a coil (see figure 3-3), so the weight is distributed over his whole chest and not just one small area. There is always a danger of cracking ribs and puncturing a lung when pulling a rope around someone's chest; this method should only be used as a last resort. The stuck caver will know immediately if this method is working or only causing damage, and you should never pull past his comfort level.

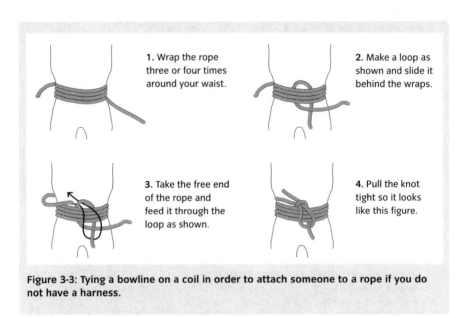

1. Wrap the rope three or four times around your waist.

2. Make a loop as shown and slide it behind the wraps.

3. Take the free end of the rope and feed it through the loop as shown.

4. Pull the knot tight so it looks like this figure.

Figure 3-3: Tying a bowline on a coil in order to attach someone to a rope if you do not have a harness.

These methods should get you out of most tight spots, but sometimes it is necessary to modify the cave to free a stuck caver. You always want to modify the weakest point that will free the person. If the floor is dirt or mud, use whatever you have to dig out the material. Sometimes simply removing a couple of rocks on the floor is enough to free the person. If the caver is stuck on a small projection, you can use a hammer or rock to break off the point.

In more extreme instances, chiseling and even blasting has been used to free stuck cavers, but only by trained rescuers. If you feel these methods are the only way you are going to get your teammate free, call for trained rescue personnel. Make sure to have someone stay with the stuck caver and try to keep him calm and comfortable until help arrives.

A caver who is stuck is likely to be more susceptible to hypothermia as well as a number of medical problems that result from poor blood circulation. A caver stuck with his head down cannot survive very long. This is a true emergency, so do not delay.

Bends

Sharp bends are an added hassle in both crawlways and squeezes. The key to getting past them is to avoid fighting the shape and natural curves of your body. If the passage turns upward, go through it on your back—that's the way your body bends. Go on your stomach if there is a sharp downward bend. If there is enough room, turn onto your right side for a sharp left bend and onto your left side for a right bend.

Tall cavers have the added limitation of long legs. Some caves feature U-turns; others, back-to-back bends like the letter Z. When you go through the first part of a Z-turn, you can bend at the waist, but as you move into the second part your knees need to bend the wrong way. While it's possible to hyperextend your knees to get through some places, it isn't advisable. In twisty, narrow passages more than 2 feet tall, try to turn onto your side and get your legs crossed Indian-style to get around the corner. This effectively shortens your legs and can help you to get through tighter bends.

Cave Packs in Small Spaces

Dealing with your cave pack in small spaces can be a big hassle. Always carry the most compact pack you can. You do need to carry your critical backup gear, clothing, food, and water, of course, but avoid bringing extra gear even if you have the space.

If you cannot wear your pack, push it in front of you. This way you have more control of it, and can easily access your gear. Most of the time you will simply push the pack ahead as you crawl. If you have a cylindrical pack, you can roll it through the passage. This is easier on your pack and takes much less energy than pushing it. Be cautious about rolling your pack down slopes where you may lose control of it. A pack rolled out of a squeeze and into a pit, stream, or narrow crack will do you no good.

In some cases, dragging your pack with an ankle may be the most efficient way to travel. In very long, low muddy or sandy crawls, you can use either the pack strap or a strong piece of webbing or rope to attach the pack to your ankle. Do not use this method in very twisty or rough passages where the pack can get hung up. If your pack snags, it will be very difficult to free unless there is someone behind you. If possible, station someone on either side of the squeeze and pass your packs through. This is usually much more efficient than making everyone struggle through with their pack.

Chimneys

A *chimney* is a narrow vertical passage or crack with walls close enough to climb if you press your feet, back, or hands against opposite walls. This opposing pressure allows you to climb even when there are no hand- or footholds. You will need to be careful when climbing up walls that are muddy or wet, however, because it will take much more pressure to give you enough friction.

The key to climbing chimneys is to always maintain three opposing points of contact with the walls. A point of contact can be a foot, knee, hand, shoulder, back, or even rear end, depending on how wide the chimney is. With three points of contact, you will not fall even if one point fails.

Basic Chimney

Note that the caver always maintains at least three contact points with the rock.

PHOTOS BY PAUL BURGER

1. The caver begins with four contact points.

2. He moves his right arm to the opposite wall, kneels on his right leg, then releases his left leg.

3. He braces against the wall with his left foot and brings his right foot down.

4. Finally, the caver holds his arms in place and works his legs downward until he can reach the floor.

Handlines

A *handline* is a rope or webbing used to make the ascent or descent of a steep passage easier, not as a substitute for climbing skills. If someone on your team would not be able to make a climb without the handline, consider rigging the rope for technical rappel and ascent—or simply skip the climb.

You need to securely anchor the rope whether you rig a handline or vertical rope. Some caves may already have anchors in place for rigging handlines; or you might find a sturdy natural anchor. Never use as a handline a rope or webbing that you would not trust your life to. Cavers sometimes get lazy about the care of ropes and decide that once a rope is no longer adequate for regular pits, it's fine for a handline. This is a mistake: A sudden fall on a handline can cause the same stresses on a rope as a vertical drop.

Most handlines are rigged so you can climb hand-over-hand down and up. You can also *arm-rappel* by running the rope across your back, wrapping your arm underneath the uphill end of the rope, and tightly grabbing the rope in your hands. If you have done this correctly, the rope should have one wrap around your upper arm. Repeat the wrap on your lower arm. Even though most of the friction will be on your upper arm, you can put a little less stress on it by wrapping your lower arm as well. Allow the rope to slide across your lower arm, back, and upper arm as you "walk" sideways down the drop. Never arm-rappel without gloves or with bare arms, unless you want serious rope burns.

This technique is good for slopes and very short, steep drops. You do not want to try this on a long, vertical drop where you are hanging free in space the whole way down.

You can *"Batman"* up the rope by leaning back with your feet flat against the rock wall and climbing the rope hand-over-hand. Obviously, this requires good upper-body strength and strong hands. You can also climb the rock on footholds while climbing the rope. Do not climb with only one hand on the rope; there is a high risk of dislocating your shoulder if you slip.

If you do not feel comfortable climbing the rope, climb the rock and have the person in front of you use the handline as a belay line. For a *belay*, the person above will use a friction device to slowly pull the rope up as you climb. In case of a fall, the belayer should be able to easily stop the rope from feeding through the friction device and keep you from falling to the ground. Establishing a proper belay and using belay devices is an advanced caving technique that should be practiced before using it in a cave. Belaying is usually taught as part of vertical caving techniques, which are covered in chapter 7.

By practicing the techniques and skills in this chapter, you should be able to handle the most common caving situations. The remaining chapters build on this knowledge and provide you with the skills needed to explore more challenging caves and situations.

HOW DO YOU MAP A CAVE?

Despite all the high-tech methods that can now be used to map the surface of the earth, the deep sea, and deep bedrock, no method has proven reliable for discovering cave passages remotely. Entrances can be seen, and there are often indications that a cave may lie below (sinkholes, vanishing streams, blowing holes), but caves cannot be mapped from the surface.

The only way to accurately map caves is by using old-fashioned compass and tape. You start at the entrance by setting a base reference point. This point—your *datum*—can be used later to tie the cave into surface features and surface maps. All the stations in the cave relate back to your datum.

Next, you find a point within sight of the first point and set this as your second station. You then measure the distance between the two points and take a compass reading from the first point to the second. In addition to the compass reading, you take an inclination with a clinometer. A *clinometer* is like an expensive, calibrated bubble level that allows you to read the slope between two points and determine how far the second station is above or below the first.

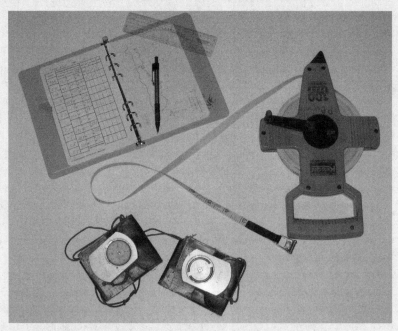

Basic cave surveying gear: surveyor's notebook with pencil and protractor, compass and clinometer, and measuring tape. PHOTO BY PAUL BURGER

Surveying in Wind Cave, South Dakota. PHOTO BY CARLETON BERN

It is important that you do not set stations on or near delicate cave formations or other sensitive cave resources. Using cave surveying instruments requires you to get very close to the station; it's easy to damage cave resources if stations are set too close.

One person on the team, the sketcher, records the data and, using a ruler and protractor, plots the points on gridded paper. She then draws a plan view to scale, showing what the cave would look like viewed from above with the roof removed. She also plots the points using the inclination data and draws a *profile,* which shows how the cave would look from the side if the walls were removed. In select places the sketcher will draw cross sections of the cave—the shape of the passage as you look down the path of travel.

The survey team then establishes a third point within sight of the second and so on, until all of the cave passages have been mapped. On the surface, the data are entered into a computer to generate a three-dimensional representation of the cave made of points and lines (survey stations and survey shots). A good, experienced team can conduct a detailed, accurate survey of a cave at the rate of 200 feet per hour.

The cartographer can then use one or several plots of these points and lines, along with the sketches from inside the cave, to generate a map of the cave. For a complex cave, the cartographer will probably break the map into multiple levels to make it easier for cavers to use. In general, it takes as long to draft a cave map as it took to map it in the first place.

TRIPS AND FALLS

ROCKFALL

GETTING LOST

HYPOTHERMIA

DEHYDRATION

BAD AIR

BAD WATER

IN CASE OF
ACCIDENT

FIRST AID

CHAPTER FOUR

Caving Hazards

Most cave accidents are minor and do not involve a cave rescue. The most frequent are injuries due to caver falls and loose rock. By knowing the hazards, however, you should be able to take fairly simple measures to avoid them.

TRIPS AND FALLS

Trips and falls are the most common type of accident in caving. You are most likely to stumble toward the end of a cave trip when you're tired and aren't picking your feet up as well as you were at the beginning. Pace yourself and keep your energy level high by eating and drinking water regularly so you can safely exit the cave. Another common cause of trips and stumbles is dim light. While it's tempting to try to squeeze the last bit of life out of a set of batteries or a charge of carbide, a dim light can make it difficult to see floor irregularities and other obstacles.

Falls are generally caused by exhaustion, carelessness, and testosterone. A climb that seemed easy on the way in can be more difficult if your energy level is low. Cavers who have spent a lot of time around pits and climbs tend to become complacent. Simply losing your balance or stepping on a rock or random piece of gear can turn even the easiest climb into a major accident site. Always be on the lookout for potential hazards around the edges of pits and climbs. Time and traffic can change climbs, and the bombproof handhold you've always used can still fail. Do not depend solely on your past knowledge of the climb; conditions may have changed.

Ego and testosterone are a significant cause of accidents, especially among experienced cavers. None of us wants to admit we're too tired to make the climb we did easily on the way in. No one wants to balk at a climb the rest of the group just completed. You will need to fight those instincts and think of your safety first. A good trip leader should make it clear from the beginning that it's okay for trip members to speak up if they're uncomfortable with a climb or any other obstacle.

As a trip leader or member, it is important that you do not try to push your fellow cavers into doing anything they think is unsafe, even if you found it trivial. Numerous accidents have occurred when a trip leader goads a novice into trying something beyond her ability. You do not want to go underground with (or be) this type of leader. There are plenty of other cavers who will be willing to take you caving. If you are uncomfortable, ask for a rope or a spotter, or opt not to do the climb. Do not let your ego, your trip leader's testosterone, or your sense of embarrassment cause an accident. It is much more embarrassing to be hauled out of a cave on a litter than to back off a climb.

Human factors are the most common cause of falls, but equipment failures can also contribute. If you are going through a cave and find a ladder, webbing, or rope already installed for a pit or climb, be very careful. As a rule, if you don't know when a piece of gear was placed in the cave and by whom, do not use it. Age, weather, and use can all cause gear to wear out. In caves frequented by novices, you may also find the wrong kind of ropes being placed by people who don't know what they're doing. Dozens of accidents have been caused by these ropes breaking, so do not trust your life to any gear that appears to be questionable. Be sure to report any such rigging or gear conditions to the appropriate person: the landowner, manager, or caving club.

If you know the rope or ladder in a particular cave is serviced regularly by a local caving club or by the agency that manages the cave, it's probably safe to assume it is in good shape. Still, do inspect the rigging and the condition of the gear, just to make sure.

ROCKFALL

Rockfall is the second most common cause of caving injuries. The entrance areas of caves are exposed to large swings in temperature, erosion, and other factors that make them especially prone to loose rocks. Many large cave rooms are littered with large, loose boulders called *breakdown*. These rocks can shift unexpectedly when you are climbing up or down. Pits with rocks at the top can be extremely hazardous given the high speeds that a falling rock can reach.

When you are in an area of loose rocks, whether it is a climb, pit, or a large pile of breakdown, be aware of people below you. If you are below an area that may pose a threat, make sure you stay out of danger, either under a ledge or far away from the rockfall zone. It is much easier to avoid rockfall completely than to count on your helmet or quick reflexes to save you from injury. Falling rocks can bounce away from the obvious fall zone, so look at the floor around you. If there is loose rock, you are probably in the rockfall zone.

If you drop or dislodge anything, whether it's a rock, debris, or even a piece of caving gear, yell *"Rock!"* to warn those below you, even if what you knocked down is very small. Small objects can dislodge larger objects, and the simple call "rock" is a clear warning to those below. Conversely, if you are on the bottom of a pit or climb and hear someone yell "rock," do not look straight up to see what is falling. Duck your head and

Large breakdown blocks. PHOTO BY STEVE REAMES

let your helmet protect you. Also, avoid the temptation to cover your head with your hands; this will only result in broken fingers.

Shifting rock can be a major hazard if the passage you are going through is between or under breakdown. If you are at all hesitant to crawl or climb in and around breakdown, don't do it. This is your brain warning you of a bad situation, even if it looks as if hundreds of people have gone before you. If you don't already know a route is safe, don't take it. Even if you are going through a breakdown passage you have been through before, it's still wise to move cautiously. Time, weathering, and traffic can all affect the stability of this type of cave passage.

In a breakdown passage, avoid pushing or kicking the rocks. The more smoothly you move, the less likely you are to dislodge a rock. Do not let your pack or clothing get snagged; if they do, don't yank on them to get them free. This may cause the rocks to shift. Never move rocks around to make the passage larger or explore some new hole. You never know which small rock is holding up the larger one above your head.

GETTING LOST

Every caver has been disoriented in a cave at least once. Even with a good map, the complex, three-dimensional nature of caves makes them difficult to navigate. Contrary to what some fans of Mark Twain may believe, leaving a long trail of string is not a good method for finding your way out of a cave. Many cavers have found tangles of line weaving in and out of passages. At the end of the string and usually only a couple of hundred feet from the entrance, you usually find an empty spool and sometimes a lost novice. Also, for the sake of the cave and those who come after you, do not leave spray-painted or chalk arrows pointing the way out. After a few people do this, these marks are both useless and bad for the cave.

Some simple guidelines can help you. First, every once in a while look behind you, especially at junctions or when entering a room. A cave passage will look different on the way out. At key junctions, pick out landmarks and try to keep them in your head like a running slideshow. Do not pick out common things as your landmarks. A random pile of dirt does not make a good landmark; use something that will stand out in your memory.

Look at the structure of the cave. Are you heading downstream on the way in, so that you'll need to head upstream on the way out? Does the rock tilt in a certain direction—and which way are you going in relation to the tilt? Is this a joint-controlled maze cave? If you know there is a regular pattern to the cave, you can probably find your way out by zigzagging in the general direction of the entrance.

Follow the wind. If you are moving through a breezy cave and feel the air in your face as you are going in, you will want to have the wind at your back on the way out. You can sometimes find the right way to go by seeing which passage has the strongest airflow. The entrance areas of cave frequently hold organic debris that has a distinctive

A typical "boneyard" maze cave. In a site like this, it's important to pick out a prominent landmark to help you remember which crawlway you came out of. PHOTO BY PAUL BURGER

smell. Sometimes it's possible to follow this smell for hundreds of feet to find your way out of a cave.

If you are in a group, keep an eye on the person in front of you and behind you. If you lose track of either, shout out so the leader can slow the pace. This simple rule will help keep the group together and prevent someone from getting lost because the team became strung out along the cave passage.

But what if none of these guidelines and tricks helps and you still end up lost? The first thing you should do is stay put. In all likelihood you are not far off the beaten path, and someone will find you. If you start to wander around, you are more likely to get further lost and will probably make it more difficult for anyone to find you. I was involved in a cave search and rescue several years ago in which a lost caver was wandering around in a large circle. Unfortunately, we rescuers were going in the same direction and did not see him. We didn't find the lost caver until he got tired and stopped, and we decided to make one more sweep of the big loop.

After you stop, put on your spare shirt and other dry, warm clothes, eat a snack, and drink a little water. If you are comfortable in the dark, turn off your light to conserve batteries. This will also make it easier to see a light passing by in the surrounding passages. If you hear someone come by, it is likely they will hear you shout; otherwise your voice probably won't carry very far. Try pounding rocks together to make noise instead of shouting yourself hoarse. This sound can be heard much farther than your voice. Do not lie down on the ground or on a rock; this will only sap your body heat. Be patient. If you are caving with a group, they will probably find you in a very short time. Otherwise your surface watch should call for help on your behalf.

HYPOTHERMIA

Hypothermia is one of the most insidious dangers in caving. Symptoms can range from simple shivering to impaired judgment and eventual death. While you are caving, it is pretty easy to stay warm. Hypothermia can set in, however, if you have to stop for a long time or if the cave is wetter than usual.

SYMPTOMS OF HYPOTHERMIA

Early Symptoms	Late Symptoms
Shivering.	The body feels cold to the touch.
Cold, pale skin.	Rigid muscles.
Lethargy and poor judgment.	Slow pulse, shallow or slower breathing.
Unsteady movements, poor balance.	Weakness, drowsiness.
Slurred speech.	Confusion.
Difficulty performing tasks, numbness.	Loss of consciousness.
	At very low body temperatures, shivering may stop.

It is much better to prevent hypothermia than to treat it once it sets in. Make sure you have the right type and amount of warm clothes for the cave you are going into (see chapter 2). Also, pack the right kinds of spare clothes in case of emergency.

If you are on a long cave trip and someone on the team needs to put on all his spare clothes in order to stay warm, it's time to leave the cave. In all likelihood, just moving will warm him up and get him out of danger. If you are in a position where a quick exit is not possible, warm him using one or more of the treatments listed below.

HYPOTHERMIA TREATMENTS

Early Treatment

If possible, get out of the cave.

Have the victim eat some food and drink water.

Remove his wet clothing and put on dry, extra clothes.

Huddle together to warm the person.

If you are using carbide or have a stove, build a heat tent.

If you have an alcohol or other stove, boil water to drink.

Do not warm the victim too quickly; this can lead to shock.

If the victim needs to urinate, let him. Otherwise, his body will use energy to keep a full bladder warm.

Late Treatment

If the person loses consciousness, immediate medical attention is needed.

If no pulse can be detected after one minute, you can perform CPR. If you can feel even a weak pulse, CPR can result in a heart attack and should not be started.

DEHYDRATION

Caving can be a strenuous activity, so it's important to drink water regularly. Dehydration can be a problem in both hot, dry caves and cold, wet ones. In caves that are very warm, you will sweat more, but the humidity does not allow your body to cool naturally. In cool, wet caves, you do not notice your thirst as much as you would in a dry cave, but you are still losing water. As the old desert hiking guidelines say, "Once you become thirsty, you are already a quart low."

Dehydration can be treated easily by drinking water, though a half-strength sports drink is better. Do not allow the dehydrated caver to drink too much too quickly or she may vomit. Severe dehydration can lead to shock, which must be treated before the dehydration. As with most caving hazards, you can prevent dehydration. Watch for the early warning signs and drink regularly.

People who are dehydrated may no longer feel hungry and may have not been eating for a long time. Make sure to eat food as well as rehydrate in order to keep energy levels up.

SIGNS OF DEHYDRATION

Mild	Moderate	Severe
Dry or sticky mouth.	Very dry mouth.	Increased thirst.
Reduced urine output.	Decreased frequency of urination (less than half your normal frequency).	Hot, dry skin—or, conversely, cold, clammy skin.
	Clumsiness or poor judgment.	Faintness that is not relieved by lying down.
	Dark, amber-colored urine.	Weak, rapid pulse.
	Faintness.	Changed mental status or severe anxiety.
	Some people experience a mild "dehydration headache."	Loss of consciousness.

BAD AIR

Bad air is defined as areas in a cave where there are low levels of oxygen or high levels of gases such as carbon dioxide or methane present. Unlike mines, most natural caves have good circulation, so bad air isn't very common.

COMMON SOURCES OF BAD AIR

- Decay of organic matter can create high levels of carbon dioxide or, more rarely, methane.
- Degassing of bat guano can create carbon dioxide and methane.
- Volcanic activity can lead to high carbon dioxide and, in some instances, hydrogen sulfide.
- Poor air circulation allows carbon dioxide to build up in the lower parts of a cave.
- Spills of chemicals or petroleum into a cave can be problematic.

Bad air can be a killer, but there are plenty of warning signs that you are getting into an area with reduced oxygen or increased carbon dioxide.

SYMPTOMS OF BAD AIR (FROM EARLY TO LATE)

Increased breathing rate.	Clumsiness.	Inability to move.
Increased pulse.	Faulty judgment.	Gasping breath.
Diminished attention span.	Rapid exhaustion.	Unconsciousness.
Dizziness.	Bad temper.	Death.
	Nausea and vomiting.	

Luckily it's easy to recognize the early warning signs of bad air and turn around. If you're not sure whether you're experiencing bad air or just becoming naturally tired, you can use a cheap lighter to test the air. At moderately low oxygen levels, the flame on a lighter or carbide lamp will change color and you will notice a small gap between the jet and the flame. The lower the oxygen level, the wider this gap will become. At levels still high enough to breathe but too low to spend much time in, the lighter will go out and cannot be relit. If your lighter goes out, leave immediately. At these low levels your judgment can become quickly impaired, and you may not notice the more advanced effects of bad air until it is too late.

Obviously, if the cave is known to have bad air caused by methane or other flammable gas, you should not use a lighter to test the air. Do not use a lighter or any open flame if you smell gasoline or another petroleum-type odor. If you go into a cave and begin to experience the early signs of bad air or smell chemical or petroleum odors, leave the cave and ask the local cavers if there are already known issues in the cave.

BAD WATER

Never assume that water in a cave is good to drink. Like surface streams, water in a cave can contain *Giardia lamblia* and other microbes that can cause diarrhea and more serious problems. Do not drink water from a cave pool or stream unless you have filtered, boiled, or otherwise treated it.

IN CASE OF ACCIDENT

If you know what to watch for, you should be able to avoid most serious accidents, but bad things are sometimes out of your control. Whether you are caving or do a lot of hiking and camping, it's a good idea to take a basic first-aid course. An advanced or wilderness first responder class is even better and will help you handle most accidents you will encounter while caving. Still, even without formal training, there are some basic things you can do.

First, stay calm and assess the situation. Make sure whatever caused the injury is not still a danger to you or the rest of your team. If the area is safe, check the injured caver in case the obvious injury is not the only one.

An injured caver with a sprain or even minor breaks can sometimes get out of the cave under his own power with some assistance. Be aware that the problem may be more serious than it appears, however, and you could be doing more harm than good by moving him through the cave on your own.

Dislocations, particularly in the shoulder, are common cave injuries. Unless you (or the caver with the dislocation) really know what you're doing, do not try to reset the joint yourself. Many people have heard you can reset a shoulder by using a bucket of water to jerk the arm back into place (or slamming it against a wall, if you're Mel Gibson); this is for a specific type of dislocation and can cause even more damage if misused. Other than stopping bleeding and preventing a condition from becoming worse, leave the medical treatment to those trained for it.

In the case of a more serious injury, you will have to call out a rescue. First, address the immediate needs of the injured. Make sure that he's out of danger from cave hazards such as rockfall, and that he's warm. Even a relatively minor injury can cause a person to go into shock.

SYMPTOMS OF SHOCK

- Cool, pale, or clammy skin.
- Thirst, nausea, or vomiting.
- Confusion or anxiety.
- Rapid, weak pulse.
- Rapid, shallow breathing.
- Faintness, dizziness, weakness.
- Loss of consciousness.

Quick treatment is the key to saving the life of someone suffering from shock. Send for help immediately and then try the following treatments until help arrives.

TREATMENT FOR SHOCK

- If there is no injury to the head, neck, or chest, place a blanket or jacket on the ground and have the victim lie down and elevate his legs about a foot above the ground. You can use a cave pack or rock to elevate the legs.
- Control any bleeding and treat any fractures or other injuries.
- Keep the person warm and comfortable with blankets, extra clothes—whatever you can find.
- If the victim vomits, turn him on his side to allow the fluids to drain.
- Talk to the person to keep him calm and reduce anxiety.

If there are four or more people on the trip, send two for help. If there are only three people on the trip, one will have to stay with the injured caver and one will have to go for help. The person leaving the cave should be the one who knows the cave the best since she will not only have to get out of the cave safely but, most likely, lead the rescuers to the accident site. A caver's first instinct is to grab her pack and run for help, but you will need to gather a bit of information first. If you have some paper and a pencil, write it down; do not rely on your memory.

Conduct a full head-to-toe assessment of the injured person, checking him for other injuries. If the injured caver is responsive, ask him if he has any additional injuries.

IMPORTANT INFORMATION TO RECORD

- Time of the accident.
- Name and age of injured.
- Overall health and fitness of injured.
- Pulse rate.
- Labored breathing or anything else out of the ordinary.
- Whether the injured caver has any kind of special medical needs, such as diabetes.
- Whether he is taking any medication, and when the last time was he took it.
- Whether he has medical allergies.
- If you have a map, mark the accident location on it.
- If you do not have a map, write down a description of the location.

Once you have all the information, you can head for the entrance. Do not rush or take any unnecessary risks to try to make the trip go faster. Remember, you are now the only link between the injured caver and the outside world. It will do him no good if you get yourself hurt trying to speed out of the cave.

When you get out, contact the appropriate emergency response agency as quickly as possible (dialing 911 on regular or cell phones will work in most places). Usually, the local or county sheriff will have jurisdiction and has contact numbers for medical people trained in cave rescue. If you come into contact with friends or relatives of the injured party, it will also be your job to keep them calm. Their first instinct will be to grab a flashlight and run into the cave. It is very easy to end up with one injured person and a handful of lost relatives in the same cave.

When the emergency personnel arrive, they are in charge of the situation and will let you know what they need from you. Although it's difficult to resist the desire to grab the nearest EMT and drag her into the cave, let the professionals do their job.

FIRST AID

You do not need advanced first-aid training in order to safely explore caves, but it will help to have some basic training to handle emergencies. Your local community college, continuing education program, or Red Cross may offer affordable classes you can take.

BASIC FIRST-AID SKILLS FOR CAVERS

CPR (cardiopulmonary resuscitation).

Dealing with cuts and other bleeding.

Dealing with broken bones, sprains, and the like.

Basic vital signs: pulse, breathing, patient assessment, and so forth.

Symptoms and treatment for hypothermia, shock, seizures, and low blood sugar.

Once you have had basic first aid and have been caving for a while, take a basic cave rescue course from the National Cave Rescue Commission (NCRC). At least once a year, this group offers a national weeklong basic cave rescue course. Throughout the year and across the country, NCRC also conducts weekend orientations to cave rescues. These courses will teach you how to handle some emergencies and show you what is involved in rescuing someone from a cave.

With the skills learned in the previous chapter and an awareness of some of the most common caving hazards, you should be well on your way to caving safely. If you practice these skills, you should be able to start exploring the more challenging caves and situations described in the chapters that follow.

Wet Caving

Many caves have streams, rivers, pools, or waterfalls, and exploring them may mean you need to spend long periods in or near water. Moving water makes communication more difficult, presents more hazards than dry caving, and can turn even minor accidents and injuries into serious situations. All water caving should be considered advanced caving and be done only with the guidance of an experienced and skilled leader.

You must take special precautions in order to keep yourself safe both prior to and during the trip, especially during emergencies. You will also need to consider your gear more carefully than you would in a dry, horizontal cave.

CLOTHING

If exploring a cave involves sections of swimming or long periods of wading, wear clothes that protect you from the water and keep you warm if you get wet. As an outer layer, wear nylon caving coveralls, a PVC suit, or a thin wet suit. Nylon suits tend to be more resistant to abrasion, particularly if you are in a cave where you will be crawling over a lot of rock or through areas with sharp projections. Depending on the exact material, nylon suits can be water-resistant but not waterproof, and most will breathe, allowing some heat and moisture to escape. PVC suits are made of material similar to rain jackets, are fairly waterproof, and are very good at keeping you dry in passages where there is a lot of dripping or in a waterfall. PVC suits keep in heat and moisture, so you may overheat if you are going to a warm or only moderately wet cave. Some nylon and PVC suit designs include a hood that can be used for additional protection and warmth. Hoods are very nice to have when climbing waterfalls and in very drippy passages.

Wet and dry suits are for serious water caving where you will be in water for most of the trip. Wet suits are designed so that your body warms a layer of water inside the suit and then keeps this warm water next to you. If you are constantly getting into and out of the water, your body will have to warm a new layer of water every time you get

Entrance to a river cave in Mexico. PHOTO BY STEPHEN LESTER

back in, sapping precious body heat and energy. Wet suits do provide added buoyancy, however, so they also make long swims easier and help you tread water.

Wet suits come in various styles and thicknesses. No matter what style you choose, make sure the wet suit is a good fit. If it's too loose, water will circulate freely and you won't stay as warm. A wet suit that is too tight, on the other hand, will constrict your movements and wear you out more quickly.

The thickness you choose will depend on your comfort level, the temperature of the cave, and how much climbing or walking you will have to do outside the stream. Thin (3 millimeter) wet suits are designed for surfing and sailboarding and will not keep you as warm as the thicker (5 mm or ¼ inch) models. On the other hand, the thinner wet suit is much more flexible and much easier to move and climb in. If you like the flexibility of the thinner wet suit, but need more warmth, wear the suit under nylon coveralls or wear a Capilene top underneath the wet suit. If you wear a nylon suit over a wet suit, the neoprene will last much longer.

If you are going to be primarily wading and not facing long sections of swimming, you can use a Farmer-John wet suit. These are neoprene bib overalls that fully cover your body up to your chest, but leave your arms uncovered. This option is warmer for wading than a 3 mm wet suit but cooler and more flexible than a full wet suit. To keep warm, wear something like a Capilene top and caving shirt over your chest and arms. Farmer-Johns are generally available only in the thicker neoprene, so walking and climbing will still be more difficult than with a thinner wet suit.

Wear socks that will keep your feet warm when wet. I have found that neoprene socks keep me the warmest and do not cause blisters on my feet the way wet wool or synthetic blends do. Consider wearing neoprene gloves under your regular caving gloves for additional protection against the cold.

For very cold caves where you will be in water for a long time, you may want to go one step farther and use a dry suit. Dry suits are completely waterproof and are designed to keep you insulated from the water. The biggest disadvantages of dry suits are that they are more expensive than wet suits and do not work well if torn or punctured. No matter what type of cave you're exploring, you will want to wear nylon or other coveralls over the dry suit to protect it. Some dry suits come with attached boots or boots and gloves designed to protect you from the water. If the dry suit boots fit into your caving boots, wear them; otherwise use wet suit neoprene socks.

To keep warm while wet caving, you will need to wear more than just caving coveralls or a wet or dry suit. Wear appropriate-weight Capilene tops under both the wet suit and coveralls, and have Capilene or wool bottoms inside the nylon or PVC coveralls. You should keep a dry Capilene top and balaclava packed so they will stay dry even if your pack gets wet. If you are not going to duck completely under the water, you can seal a balaclava in a resealable sandwich bag and store it above the suspension in your helmet. You can also store extra clothes inside a one-liter widemouthed water bottle; this will keep them dry even under extreme water conditions.

CAVE PACKS

There are several factors to consider when choosing a pack for wet caving, as well as when packing the items inside it. No cave pack is completely waterproof by itself, but most of the time that doesn't matter. The amount of water your pack absorbs and holds will affect how much weight you have to carry and how buoyant you are when swimming. PVC packs do not absorb water, so they'll weigh about the same wet as they do dry. Nylon absorbs more water than PVC, but still less than any of the canvas or denim packs.

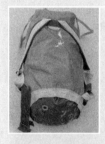

Expedition caving pack with drain holes in the bottom.
PHOTO BY PAUL BURGER

A dry bag can keep gear from getting wet inside an expedition caving pack.
PHOTO BY PAUL BURGER

A waterproof cave drum fits inside an expedition pack to keep gear dry.
PHOTO BY PAUL BURGER

Regardless of the type of material you choose, make sure there is some kind of drain hole so you are carrying as little water weight as possible. Most PVC and nylon caving packs have a grommet hole or something similar on the bottom, so that when the pack gets submerged it drains easily. Fanny packs, backpacks, gas mask bags, and other packs you buy at regular outdoor equipment stores will not have drain holes. Grommet kits are cheap and easy to use and provide a good drain hole without compromising the integrity of the pack.

There are ways to keep gear completely dry. For extra clothes or small items, the cheapest way is to pack them into a one-liter, widemouthed bottle. If your gear is too large to fit into a bottle, you can buy a dry bag that fits into your pack. These bags are used by kayakers and rafters to keep gear dry on river trips. Pack the dry bag about two-thirds full with something relatively soft on top and then fold the top of the bag down several times. Most dry bags have a buckle to hold the bag closed once it is rolled up. Dry bags are very effective at protecting gear, but you should pack your emergency clothes into a resealable sandwich bag, too, just in case. Dry bags can leak if you force your pack underwater. This generally happens when you are using your pack as a flotation device on a long swim.

There are several expedition caving and camping duffel bags designed to hold waterproof plastic drums. These drums have an O-ring to seal the lid, provide a lot of buoyancy, and protect equipment fairly well. A disadvantage is that you have to pack carefully so that the one item you need is not buried at the bottom of the bottle. It can also be a hassle getting the drums to fit easily into cave duffels.

To keep cameras and other equipment completely dry, you can use a Pelican case or similar waterproof box. These cases come in many different sizes and have a foam insert that can be custom-cut to fit almost any type of equipment. A neoprene gasket makes a tight seal when the box is closed and latched. The biggest disadvantage is that even good used cases are very expensive.

Large and small waterproof boxes carry photo gear, scientific instruments, and surveying instruments.
PHOTO BY PAUL BURGER

Buoyancy is vital to safe river caving. Swimming with packs that are too heavy and not buoyant can not only slow you down, but even lead to drowning. This is especially important to consider when you are carrying large amounts of vertical caving equipment or other heavy items.

Your pack should help keep you afloat; it should be unable to sink to the bottom of a deep pool or underground river. Your gear will do you very little good lost in the murk of a cave pool, and you will tire yourself and become hypothermic diving for it.

The large containers and waterproof boxes, and to some extent dry bags, are naturally buoyant because it is nearly impossible to fill all the space. If you are not using any of these, there are other things you can do to make your pack buoyant. Carry one or two empty water bottles to increase buoyancy. You also can use empty plastic soda pop bottles or the liner from a box of wine. These are generally tough and light, and they can be adjusted by inflating or deflating.

If you are unsure how much buoyancy you need, pack up your equipment before the trip and test it in the bathtub or a barrel of water. Once you get into the cave, it's difficult to make your pack more buoyant, and it's unsafe to swim or negotiate deep water with a pack that can be lost or pull you under.

If you cannot swim, do not count on your pack alone to keep you afloat. Wear a life vest or other personal flotation device.

EMERGENCY EQUIPMENT

If you are going to a wet cave, it's important to bring extra clothes or something to keep you warm in case of an emergency. As mentioned before, you can carry a dry balaclava in a plastic bag in your helmet lining or a dry Capilene top in a water bottle. If you do not have the space for an extra water bottle, pack a garbage bag or foil emergency blanket. Either can be used to make a heat tent. The bag or blanket will trap your heat, and if you have a candle or carbide lamp, you can put it inside with you for added warmth. In addition to trapping your heat, bags and emergency blankets will also trap moisture that condenses inside and could make you wetter. It may be necessary to shake out the bag or blanket from time to time to keep this condensation from raining down on you.

As mentioned in chapter 2, you may want to bring a small alcohol or heat tab stove that can be used to heat water or small cans of food. You would be surprised how much a drink of hot water or bite of warm food will reinvigorate a team on a long, wet trip. Just remember that a can with the lid closed will act as a pressure cooker, heating more quickly than an open can. Be careful not to overheat the can, which could explode and send scalding food over you and the cave.

A short piece of 1-inch tubular webbing can handle many types of emergencies. Fifty feet of webbing doesn't take up too much room and can be used for water crossings and short canals, steep or muddy slopes, and short waterfalls; it can also be used as a pack tether when you swim in deep water. Webbing can be used as a rescue line if someone is having problems swimming or to help support someone who is jammed in a crack.

SPECIAL PRECAUTIONS

Water caves are dynamic and unpredictable—that's what makes them fun to explore. It can also make them dangerous, however, if you do not take special care. Bringing the right equipment is only part of being prepared. It's even more important to watch for the signs of trouble before you get into the cave.

A review of the past fifteen years of *American Caving Accidents*, published by the National Speleological Society, shows that the vast majority of nondiving water caving emergencies were caused by flooding. The primary cause of nearly all of these was a team entering the cave during bad weather. Get the forecast and know the weather conditions *before* you head into a cave with a river or stream. Even if the forecast shows that the weather is going to be clear, if you get to the cave and it looks like it may rain, do not enter the cave.

Some caves and passages will flood all the way to the ceiling, while others become only temporarily blocked and still have air-filled passages, even in flood stage. It's important to learn as much as you can about the dynamics of a particular cave from experienced cavers, publications, and observing features in the cave. You can frequently see old flood lines or places where sticks, logs, and other debris have been jammed into the ceiling of passages by past floods.

Some caves flood only during heavy spring runoff or in very strong storms, but you have no way of knowing how powerful an upcoming storm may be. Even cavers who know a cave and how it reacts to storms have been caught in dangerous flooding conditions when their best judgment was to continue the trip. Again, your safest bet is to stay out of any wet caves if there is a possibility of rain.

If you go into a wet cave, make sure everyone on the trip is prepared and has the emergency supplies described in the previous section. All of you should know exactly what conditions you're likely to encounter, and should be confident you'll be able to handle those conditions. You don't want to be faced with a long swim only to discover that one of the people on your team can't swim. Never assume everyone on the trip knows what they are getting into.

Before going into the cave, make sure to look at a cave map or get a good description of places you can go in case of a flood or if you just need to get out of the water. Find out if there are alternative higher exits and how to reach them in case of emergency. Being prepared with the right gear and information is the best ammunition you have against an emergency. In many cases you won't be able to exit the cave until the floodwaters recede.

Make sure your surface watch knows your route through the cave as well as your expected exit time. If there is an emergency and you are forced to stay in the cave until water subsides, rescuers will need to know where in the cave you planned on going, when you planned on entering the cave, and when you planned on exiting. With this information and knowledge of the cave, they can predict where in the cave you are and where you may be waiting out the flood. This will also give them information so they can reach you via alternate routes you may not know about. The dangers of a water cave and the high potential for hypothermia make it vital that you have a good, knowledgeable surface watch so that rescue can come quickly.

TECHNIQUES

A cave with flowing water is more challenging than a dry, horizontal cave. You may encounter poor footing, deep or fast-moving water, waterfalls, and other obstacles. You will also be carrying more gear and be dressed more restrictively than usual. Experience in many different water caves, and repeated visits to the same cave, will help you learn how to move safely and efficiently. The techniques described here will help you get a head start.

Moving through water is a lot of work and will sap your energy and body heat quickly. It's best to stay out of the water for as long as you can, even if you are feeling overheated at the beginning of a trip. Resist the temptation to start wading or swimming before you absolutely need to. Wet caves are exciting, and it always seems like more fun to be in the water than out, but you need to pace your energy and warmth for the whole trip.

Mud Banks

If you do a lot of wet caving, you will eventually have to cross or climb the mud banks that tend to form along the edge of a stream. In some cases these banks are gently sloping and wide, making them very easy to walk along. Unfortunately there will come a time when you have to walk along a steep mud bank or climb up one in order to get out of the water. Done correctly, this is generally not difficult, but done incorrectly you may end up taking an inadvertent swim, to the almost certain amusement of your friends.

If you have to traverse a mud bank and there isn't already a trail across it, you need to create a ledge by kicking steps or a narrow path into the mud. If you pick a route too close to the water, the mud may be saturated and too weak to support your weight. Do not pick a route that is so high on the bank that a fall could result in serious injury. If you are kicking steps, remember that not everyone who comes after will have legs as long as you; don't make the steps too far apart. This could cause the next caver to lose his balance and end up in the water. If the team is already wet, the water from their boots and clothes will make the path more slippery with each person who crosses.

You may want to rig a traverse line or handline if the bank is steep and there are dangerous obstacles below, such as a long drop or swift water. You will need good, solid anchors and will need to keep the rope or webbing taut. If the rope is too slack, a caver taking a fall could still end up in the water or hanging far down on the mud bank.

Be very careful when you first encounter a steep mud slope from the top. If you have rope or webbing, it's a good idea to rig a safety line for a first descent. You have no way of knowing how fast the current might be or how stable the mud bank, and you don't want to slide uncontrollably into the water.

Stream Crawls

Many wet passages are too low to stoop or walk through. The techniques for going through a stream crawl are the same as those used in a dry crawl and will depend on the height and width of the passage. Keep your chest and head out of the water as much as possible since this is where your body loses the most heat. Make sure you wear appropriate clothing and that your caving suit is closed all the way to the top.

Wading

If a stream is clear and its floor smooth, wading is simple. Unfortunately, this is rarely the case. Unless you're at the head of the line and the mud has not yet been stirred up, you will most likely be unable to see the floor of the stream; you'll have to go by feel. As you move, slide your feet forward just above the floor. This will allow you to feel for obstacles such as submerged rocks or logs. You will also need to step carefully so you do not step into any holes. If you do encounter a hidden rock or other obstacle, be sure to warn the cavers behind you.

Swims

Swimming can be one of the most fun—yet also challenging—activities you can do in a cave. Most people are used to swimming in pools, river, lakes, and oceans, usually in just a bathing suit or wet suit. Swimming with heavy caving gear while wearing caving clothes makes it more difficult and more dangerous. Never attempt to swim across fast-moving water without a safety line. You can be easily swept over waterfalls, through rapids, or into deep pools, or become trapped under rocks.

If you do not know how to swim, use some kind of personal flotation device or do not go into the water. Stream caving is unforgiving of even small mistakes, and you will put the rest of your team at risk trying to rescue you.

Your buoyancy is the number one factor to consider. No amount of strength will allow you to swim in deep water if your gear and clothing are too heavy. As described in "Cave Packs," there are many things you can do to make your pack more buoyant, including packing your gear in a dry bag or inside plastic containers and carrying air-filled containers.

If your pack is buoyant enough and large enough, it can be used as a flotation device. Usually only large camp duffels are big enough to work well, because they have enough buoyancy to support a person. Simply wrap your arms around the pack, grasp your hands underwater as if you were giving your pack a hug, and use your feet to kick through the water. Be careful if you are using a dry bag for your gear. If you force a dry bag under the water, it may leak, get your gear wet, and cause you to lose buoyancy.

If you are carrying a small pack, you'll probably need to swim on your own, without using your pack as flotation. Any swimming stroke that puts your head underwater (such as the crawl) is not useful in a cave. You need to keep your head above water in order to stay warm, to see, and to keep your headlamp from getting damaged. (Hopefully your headlamp is reasonably waterproof.)

The breaststroke is energy-efficient, and you can do it while keeping your head out of the water. It's also a good stroke for moving through areas with low airspace, since it can be done without making large waves. One disadvantage is that holding your head out of the water for extended periods will make your neck tired. The sidestroke can also be effective, especially if you need a free arm to carry your pack. If you use the sidestroke, however, you will get your head partially wet and will get cold more quickly.

If you know you are going to have to swim for long distances and do not have a large, buoyant pack, you may want to use an external flotation device. Life jackets and similar devices can be used effectively in a cave. If you will be in a strong current of

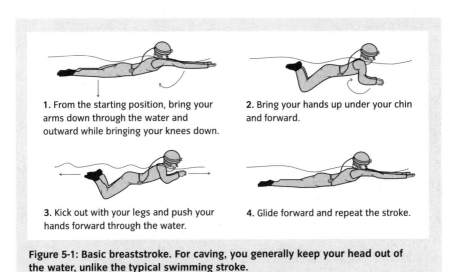

1. From the starting position, bring your arms down through the water and outward while bringing your knees down.

2. Bring your hands up under your chin and forward.

3. Kick out with your legs and push your hands forward through the water.

4. Glide forward and repeat the stroke.

Figure 5-1: Basic breaststroke. For caving, you generally keep your head out of the water, unlike the typical swimming stroke.

water going downstream, float with your feet up in front of you. Try not to drag your feet on the bottom. Your boot could become jammed between rocks; it's easy to twist an ankle, or worse. In calm water, swim backward. If you swim facedown and forward, your life jacket will ride high and push up around your face, and you will have to fight to keep from flipping over onto your back. In rapid water, never float downstream head-first. You risk serious head injury and increase your risk of drowning.

You can also use a kickboard for long swims. These light, simple devices are usually used to help beginner swimmers concentrate on training leg strength. You grab the edges of the gravestone-shaped board, put your chest on the flat surface, and move forward by kicking your legs. For very long swims with a kickboard, you may consider using a pair of swim fins to maximize your efficiency. If you do choose to wear fins, make sure you have regular boots or thick-soled neoprene boots for crossing stretches of land, rimstone dams, and shallow water. Fins are very awkward to walk in.

Rafts and Inner Tubes

There are several ways to cross long stretches of deep water—indeed, any water passage—without getting wet. The most obvious is to use an inflatable raft. Pick one that's relatively compact, does not require a special pump, and is made of very tough material such as neoprene. The tougher the raft, of course, the heavier it will be. And no matter how tough yours is, you'll need to be careful about rubbing its sides or bottom on a cave's walls and floor. Make sure you have a repair kit, especially if the raft is going to be left in the cave between trips.

Getting into an inflatable raft can be a tricky and amusing business. You want to keep your center of gravity as low as possible. Put your pack in first.

As you paddle, use only your arms outside the boat. If you lean out so your chest is over the water, you're likely to flip the raft. This is even more tricky if there are two people: Make sure you don't both lean out in the same direction while paddling.

Inner tubes are generally lighter than rafts and easier to get in and out of. If you sit in the center of an inner tube, you will get your legs and behind wet. A variation on the basic inner tube has a set of waders built in so your legs will hang down into the water, but you won't get wet. These are normally used by anglers in deep, still water and are available at many fishing equipment stores. You can also buy an inner tube with a harness or rig your own harness using webbing. In Europe this type of inner tube setup is called a *buoy*.

You would use separate chest waders in a buoy or purchase a set of lighter, more flexible caving chest waders (called a *pontonnière* in Europe and not widely available in the United States). With the waders on, you step into the harness so your legs hang below the inner tube. Your center of gravity is naturally very low in this setup, and it is very difficult to flip over. You will want to remove the waders when you are not using them since your sweat will build up on the inside and make you wet.

| 1. Place your left hand on the front of the raft and your left knee on the raft's inside left. Stay as low as possible. | 2. Bring your right hand to the front of the raft. | 3. Bring your other leg into the raft so that both knees are pressed against the inside. |

Figure 5-2a: Getting into a raft along the shore.

| 1. Bring the raft along-side you. | 2. Pull up on the wall and swing your left leg into the raft. Use your leg to hold the raft steady. | 3. Bring your right leg into the raft and put your knees along the inside edge. Let go of the wall and bring your hands to the sides of the raft. |

Figure 5-2b: Getting into a raft in deep water.

Low Airspaces

In almost any wet cave, you will encounter a low airspace—a place where the water comes almost up to the ceiling. You may not be able to see far enough ahead to tell if the airspace closes up completely (sumps) or it's possible to get through. First, feel if there is any wind coming through. If the wind is getting through, then the passage is not sumped. You can also send a wave of water down the passage and listen to the sound it makes. If it makes a hollow clunking or sucking sound, the passage is most likely sumped. You'll have to return when the water is lower.

A stream passage with a low airspace. Note that the rope is used as a guideline; there's debris on the ceiling from seasonal flooding.
PHOTO BY PAUL BURGER

When the water is sumped behind a rimstone dam, a sand bank, or rocks, it may be possible to lower the sump. In the case of sand or loose rocks, you can dig out a trench to let the water out and lower the water level. With a rimstone dam or bedrock feature holding the water back, you can use a bucket to bail water or use a short length of hose to siphon the water level down.

If you use a siphon, be careful not to sump the passage behind you by draining the pool in front of you. Many stream passages are made up of a series of pools with low airspaces above them. By emptying one upstream, you could sump the passage behind you and block the way out.

If the passage is not sumped, there are several techniques for getting through. Obviously, if you're using a carbide light, you will need to use a water-resistant electric backup since water will put out the flame and leave you in the dark. The most important things to remember, especially in a large group, are: Don't make waves, and don't panic. If you are going through a very low airspace and someone behind or in front of you makes a wave, you are likely to get water in your nose or mouth and start to panic. Once you do, your fleeing instincts will kick in (even though you have no place to go), your breathing rate will increase, and you will probably end up sucking in more water. Make sure everyone on the team knows to not make waves, and try to keep the cavers around you calm.

If the airspace is more than a foot high, you can probably just crawl, walk, or breast-stroke through, depending on the total height of the cave passage. Adjust your head-lamp to shine down the passage and not on the water surface or wall. This will make it easier to follow turns in the cave passage ahead, see obstacles, and know how far you have to go before the passage opens up again.

A typical ear duck in a passage with low airspace.
PHOTO BY PAUL BURGER

Ear Duck

When the airspace is less than a foot high, you will probably have to do an *ear duck* to get through. Turn your head sideways and make sure your headlamp is angled so it shines down the passage. Push ahead with your head partially in the water, breathing either through your nose or through part of your mouth. Depending on how small the airspace is, you will get anything from just an ear to half of your head wet doing the ear duck.

When you immerse your ears in cold water, it can negatively affect your equilibrium and make you stagger like a drunk caver. If you feel a little dizzy, wait a few seconds before you keep going. The effect will last only until your head warms back up a little.

Headfirst Ceiling Suck

When there are only a couple of inches of airspace, you will have to do a *ceiling suck* to get through. All ceiling suck methods involve getting your face as close to the ceiling as possible and pursing your lips so you can breathe in the limited airspace. Most of the time you will want to remove your helmet so you can get your face closer to the ceiling.

To do the headfirst ceiling suck, roll over onto your back and bring your face up to the ceiling. Carefully move into the low airspace headfirst, being careful not to make any waves. You can stretch your arms out behind you to feel for the way and help pull yourself through the passage. When using this method, it is best to keep your eyes closed to prevent mud and other ceiling debris from getting in them. Since you cannot see forward anyway, there is no good reason to have your eyes open. In some cases the airspace may be so low that the water covers your eyes as well as your head.

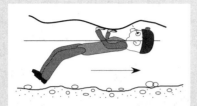

Figure 5-3a: Headfirst ceiling suck. The arrow indicates the direction of travel.

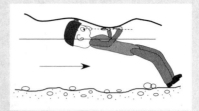

Figure 5-3b: Feetfirst ceiling suck. The arrow indicates the direction of travel.

Feetfirst Ceiling Suck

The feetfirst ceiling suck is basically the same as the headfirst variety except that you walk or move forward with your feet out in front of you, depending on how large the passage is. Using this method without your helmet, it is sometimes possible to pivot your chin down while holding your breath to get a look at the passage ahead. If you can see ahead from time to time, it makes it easier psychologically to keep going and may help you pick a shorter route through the low airspace.

Duck-Under

In some caves the route goes through a short passage that is almost always sumped. It's sometimes possible to do a *duck-under* or free dive to get through a short sump. Never attempt a free dive unless you know how long the sump is and have been through with someone intimately knowledgeable about it. Never attempt a duck-under with someone who cannot swim or has a fear of water.

Even if you or someone on your team has been through the duck many times, remember that stream passages are dynamic. Floods can fill passages with sand and gravel or bring other debris into a cave. You do not want to swim into the base of a log-jam or get stuck partway through.

In general, you should take three deep breaths before going underwater. Move steadily and smoothly through the passage until you emerge on the far side. Be careful not to surface into an *air bell*—a place where the ceiling rises enough to be free of water. Carbon dioxide can build up in air bells, and if you enter one and inhale, it can be deadly.

On short duck-unders you may be able to reach through from the far side to help pull the next caver through. This is especially useful for beginning cavers and will help their confidence.

Some frequently used duck-under passages have fixed ropes (guidelines) running through them to make getting through easier. There should be enough slack in the line that you can hand-over-hand the rope and pull yourself quickly through.

You will not be able to communicate through the sump. Work out *all-clear* signals ahead of time, such as a fixed number of strong tugs, so you'll know when someone is through the duck. You don't want to accidentally have more than one person at a time on the line underwater. Before you use a line, give it a tug or shake to make sure no one else is using it. Pull yourself steadily and smoothly through the water until you emerge back into the air-filled cave passage.

Unlike most water caving situations, you *don't* want to be very buoyant going through a duck-under. It will take a lot of effort to get through the water if you are jammed against the ceiling or dragging against the bottom. Try to adjust your buoyancy so that you float just above the bottom. There are many dangers to traversing a duck-under, so only attempt it after you have gained a lot of experience in water caving and are with an experienced, competent guide.

Waterfalls

Waterfalls can be one of the most exciting and dangerous obstacles in water caving. Whether the waterfall is a free climb or needs to be rigged with rope, you want to try to stay out of the water as much as possible. It will be difficult to find foot- and handholds under a steady flow, and the force of the water will try to push you off the climb. The action of the water can weaken holds and make the climb more dangerous. It is also a good idea to stay out of the water to conserve your body heat.

When you come to the top of a waterfall and need to climb down, try to pick a route that keeps you out of the water as much as possible. In a narrow waterfall passage, chimney out, away from the waterfall, and then climb down to the floor.

If you have no option but to climb directly down the flow, rig a handline so you can lean out while descending with your feet against the wall and keep your chest and upper body out of the water. With a handline you may be able to swing out, completely away from the flow, where you could not free climb. Before you climb, make sure your caving suit is closed and your hood is up (if you have a suit with a hood) to minimize the amount of water that can reach your skin.

If you are rigging the waterfall with a rope for technical descent and ascent, use an anchor that keeps the rope out of the path of the water. In some cases, you may need to set a bolt or a series of bolts out, away from the waterfall, to rig out of the water. If there is no way to rig out of the waterfall due to lack of gear or anchors, you will need to either use your feet to keep you out of the water or make sure you are dressed appropriately to handle getting wet.

Before you climb, make sure everyone closes up their suits and pulls up their hoods. If you don't have a hood, you can use a garbage bag as a makeshift hood or rain jacket by tearing a hole in one corner and slipping it over your head. Make sure the bag does not interfere with the smooth, safe operation of your ascending gear; you may want to wear the bag inside your shirt or suit.

Put the least experienced caver in the middle of the group so if she gets in trouble on rope, there will be people both above and below to assist. Getting in trouble partway up a waterfall drop can become deadly very quickly, so make sure everyone on the team is prepared to handle a wet vertical drop. Everyone must be dressed against the cold as well.

Plunge Pools

A *plunge pool* is a special type of waterfall passage where there is relatively deep water at the bottom of the drop. There are many places where cavers will jump into the deep water, sometimes even drops in excess of 30 feet. While this can be exhilarating, it is also very dangerous. There is no way of knowing how deep the water is, if there are submerged rocks or other hazards, or if there is a strong current or undertow. Even if you have jumped into a plunge pool dozens of times, water caves are dynamic and you have no way of knowing if debris has washed into the pool or if it has been filled with sand. There have been many cases of broken bones and other serious injuries from cavers jumping into water that was too shallow or from landing on a large rock barely submerged in the pool.

When you get to a plunge pool, do not jump in unless a caver in front of you has already checked the depth of the pool and made sure there are no submerged hazards. You will always be better off climbing down the drop as far as possible before jumping. If you are entering deep water for the first time, make sure you're buoyant enough to float and your gear is securely attached.

It will be nearly impossible to keep anything but your head completely dry in a plunge pool, so be sure you have clothing that will keep you warm for the rest of the trip. You will also want warm, dry clothes in your pack in case of emergencies or if the trip is going to be very long.

Water Crossings

Many stream caves require you to cross fast-moving water to reach the far bank or a side lead. Most of the time you can simply wade through the stream, bracing yourself on submerged rocks or the streambed. If there is any danger of being swept downstream, however, you need to set up a belay or traverse line.

To set up a belay, use a half hitch to attach a rope or webbing to the wrist of the caver who is going to cross. Walk downstream along the bank, letting out enough rope to span the stream. The lead caver should cross the stream, letting the current help move him forward. If he slips or cannot cross the current, he will simply float downstream and the belay line will pull him to shore. For a deep-water crossing, you want the lead caver to be the strongest swimmer. Make sure he has a life jacket or other flotation device.

Once the lead caver is on the other side, you can either belay the remainder of the team across or rig a traverse line. To set up a traverse line, you need to make sure that it's rigged so you aren't trying to cross against the current, and that the anchors on both sides are strong. There should be as little slack in the line as possible. The caver will clip into the traverse line with her harness and pull herself across. If you are using a traverse line without a seat harness, use a belay on the person crossing the stream.

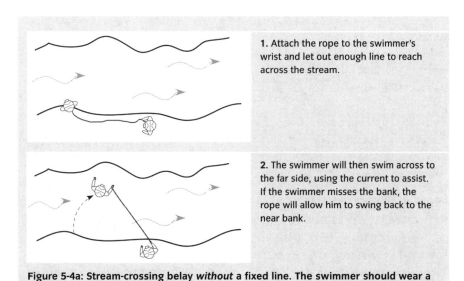

1. Attach the rope to the swimmer's wrist and let out enough line to reach across the stream.

2. The swimmer will then swim across to the far side, using the current to assist. If the swimmer misses the bank, the rope will allow him to swing back to the near bank.

Figure 5-4a: Stream-crossing belay *without* a fixed line. The swimmer should wear a life vest or other flotation device.

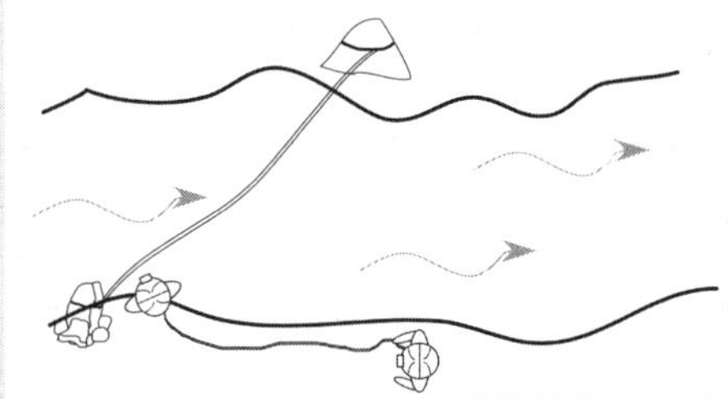

1. Attach the rope onto the swimmer's wrist and let out enough line to reach across the stream. The fixed line should be rigged so that the swimmer is not fighting the current.

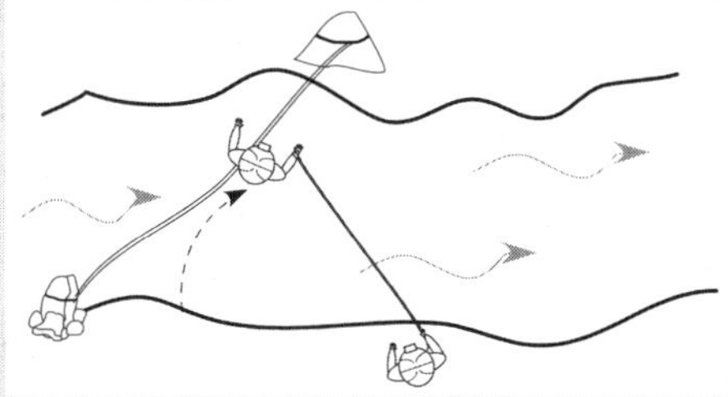

2. The swimmer will attach her seat harness to the fixed line and use either her hands or an ascender to cross the stream.

Figure 5-4b: Stream-crossing belay *with* a fixed line. The swimmer should wear a life vest or other flotation device.

Canals

Canals are sections of stream passage with strong currents and sheer bedrock walls. Small canals with slower currents can usually be traversed by swimming, walking along the bottom, or holding on to the wall. In fast-moving water you must rig a canal line.

A *canal line* is a fixed rope rigged along the length of the passage. It is used to guide you downstream and help pull you upstream. On longer canals it will likely be a series of lines anchored to the rock. When you travel downstream, you clip your cowstail into the line and move from anchor to anchor. To travel upstream you can either hand-over-hand the rope while you are attached with your cowstail, or use an ascender to pull yourself along.

Fighting a strong current using a canal line will sap your strength and your body heat, and you could become trapped downstream. In a very large stream or river canal with a strong current, it's best to rig completely out of the water with a series of Tyrolean traverses.

Ropes in Water Passages

Some cavers prefer to use polypropylene rope (similar to that used for waterskiing) instead of nylon to rig canals, stream crossings, and guidelines. Polypropylene rope floats and isn't as prone to tangling in swift water as nylon rope, but it's not as strong, either. Nylon rope is more difficult to deal with in water passages because it doesn't float, but it's very strong. Except in very special circumstances, use nylon rope or webbing for rigging.

Polypropylene rope is good for tethering packs or other gear in a wet cave because it floats, making it easy to find the line if you need to lift your pack or recover it from a pool. It's also good for attaching water bottles or other gear to your harness.

Some caves have semipermanent lines rigged in them. As with ropes in dry, horizontal caves, never depend on lines you do not know the history of. Passages that are prone to flooding or that have strong currents can wear out rope quickly. Sometimes there will be very little noticeable wear on a rope even though most of its strength is gone. Water can also wear out bolts and other anchors, so even if you are confident in the line, check the anchors before using them.

HAZARDS AND WATER EMERGENCIES

Wet caves have their own unique hazards and require special skills. Observation and preparation can prevent most accidents and keep you out of dangerous situations. The most dangerous environmental hazard is inappropriate clothing. The physical hazards are slippery, wet mud and other slick surfaces, underwater obstacles, and high water.

Slippery or Deep Mud

Most stream caves have some mud or clay deposits. Previously I described how to deal with slippery mud banks using steps kicked into the surface, handlines, and even ice tools. Nonsloping mud can be just as slippery as a steep mud bank, however, so choose your footing carefully. You will not need to rig a traverse line or any other kind of protection, but you should walk carefully, especially if your boots are already wet.

Cave mud poses a risk even once you are out of the muddy passage. If the bottoms of your boots are covered in mud, it will make climbing and scrambling over rocks much more difficult. When you get out of a muddy passage, try to clean the soles of your boots in the cave stream or against a rock. Choose a rock that will be washed clean the next time the cave floods. Before you climb or start across breakdown or bedrock floors, check your boots to make sure there is no mud on the soles. Also, make sure that your gloves are clean so you don't lose your grip on the rope.

Mud on your boots isn't only a safety hazard, but can also cause quite a bit of impact on the rest of the cave. You can track mud through relatively clean areas, covering flowstone or other formations. Or it can get tracked into clean pools and disrupt wildlife. It is important to be aware of what you are carrying from passage to passage on your boots and clothing.

If you are walking through a passage with very deep mud, it is possible to get your boot stuck. You can lose a boot in deep mud, but can also dislocate or sprain your knee or ankle trying to pull free. If your foot gets stuck in deep mud, stop moving forward immediately. Pull it out slowly while holding on to the top of your boot. If a slow, steady pull doesn't work, rock your foot and leg forward and back to make a larger hole for your foot to come out.

Underwater Obstacles

Potholes, leg holds, snags, and other hidden underwater obstacles are all common beneath cave waters. *Potholes* are places in the stream floor where water has carved a hole in the bedrock or washed sediment away. They can range in size from just large enough to twist or break an ankle to large enough to fall into completely. At best, cavers will be embarrassed as they walk casually into a pothole and sink in over their heads. At worst, they can get wedged completely underwater. If this happens, it is usually easy to pull the victim back out by the arms or clothing, but you will need to act quickly.

Be careful with your gear near potholes. If you lose something in a pothole, you will have to abandon it or try to reach it by lying in the stream. You do not want to dive headfirst into a pothole; there is too much chance you will get stuck, be injured, or even drown.

Another type of hazard, *leg holds*, are small potholes or cracks underwater that can grab a foot or leg. If this happens, there is a serious risk of twisting or breaking your ankle. It is also possible to slip and become jammed in a leg hold underwater or in a place where the force of the water can push you under. If you are in a situation where your foot is jammed and there is no danger of drowning, you can try to free your foot by moving it forward and back. You can also simply remove your boot and slide out.

If there *is* immediate danger of drowning, you may need to rig a line around the stuck caver's chest to keep her head above the water. Once she's secure, someone else on the team can try to free the stuck foot or remove the boot. It's critical to work quickly to prevent exhaustion and hypothermia.

Snags are places where logs, branches, or other debris have piled up in the streambed. It's easy to step between or slip off submerged snags and injure an ankle or leg. A solid-looking log can be rotten or weak after being submerged for a long time.

The best way to avoid underwater hazards is to walk carefully and step down only when you are sure of the footing. If you do get your ankle or leg stuck, stop moving forward and free it. Do not try to keep moving at a fast pace and just pull it free.

Flooding

Flooding is the most serious danger to explorers in active stream caves. As I mentioned earlier, the best way to prevent getting caught in a flood is to know the cave and the weather. Do not enter a cave that has an active stream if it's raining, if the forecast calls for storms, or if the water looks unusually high when you get to the cave.

There are times when the unexpected happens and the water begins to rise in a cave. You may actually see the water rise, but usually it's a gradual process and hard to notice in the excitement of caving. In a flood you will notice that a waterfall or stream is suddenly louder. Also look for the sudden appearance of a lot of sticks, leaves, and other debris in the water. The water may turn muddy as it rises. All these signs of flood tell you to act quickly.

Never enter a cave stream or waterfall that is flooding in an attempt to get out. The water only has to be knee-deep to sweep you away. Unless you can see daylight and know the current isn't too strong, it is unlikely you will be able to beat the rising water level and reach the entrance. Do not panic. Head for higher ground and wait for the water to subside. If you have prepared correctly for the trip, you have identified areas in the cave that are above the active stream level and would make good refuges.

When you are safely out of the flood zone and as high in the passage as you can get, huddle together with your companions to keep warm and conserve your body heat. Eat a snack and drink a little water to keep your body's furnace cranked up. Conserve your lights and other resources; you don't know how long you may have to wait. In time the water level will drop or your surface watch will have notified emergency response personnel that you are overdue.

If you are in a vertical stream cave and have left ropes rigged, be very careful once you start climbing back out. The floodwaters or debris may have damaged your ropes or anchors, and they may no longer be safe to climb. Test the ropes by getting several people to put their weight on the bottom. Even if the rope holds under this weight testing, climb carefully. If you have any doubts, wait for a rescue and concentrate on keeping warm and dry.

In the event the cave starts flooding while you are on rope, you'll have to quickly judge whether it will be faster to continue the climb or to change over and descend. Consider where the rest of your team is and try to make sure everyone is together. You also need to determine if your best place of refuge from high water is above or below the drop.

There will be cases when it's best to head out of the cave, but that call should be made by someone very experienced with the cave and river caving in general. The leader should know the limitations of the team and base the decision on those abilities and how well prepared everyone is to handle the new caving conditions.

Exploring wet caves can be exciting, but can also be one of the most hazardous and least forgiving types of caving. You must be aware of conditions both on the surface and underground and always be on the lookout for signs that those conditions are changing. Put simply, all wet caving should be considered advanced caving; always go with an experienced caver as your leader.

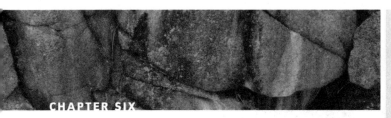

Trip Organization and Leadership

If you are an experienced caver, this chapter will help you organize trips, recognize different caving styles, and learn to deal with team problems during a cave trip. If you are a beginner, you will learn what goes into planning and running a cave trip, discover the qualities of a good trip leader, and understand what it takes to be a good team member.

WHY TRAINING TRIPS?

Many experienced cavers are hesitant to lead training trips, thinking their time is better spent exploring or working on their own projects. Yet the cavers we train today will be the ones who will continue these projects in the future. If we do not train them, they will waste time and effort relearning what we already know. This is inefficient and causes a great deal of unnecessary damage to caves.

Even if everyone on a training trip does not become an avid caver, you are giving people an understanding of why caves are important. The more people appreciate the unique resources of caves, the easier it will be for cavers to gain public support in protecting cave and karst resources. A small effort on your part can make a big difference.

Many new cavers do not want to participate in a series of training trips but prefer to jump straight into the "good stuff." If you skip training trips and avoid organized caving groups as a beginner, however, you will be missing out on valuable information and insight. You cannot get this information and training from the Internet or any caving book.

Be patient and understanding with experienced cavers as you're starting out. They have no idea what your skills are or how well you will do underground, so they have to

[left] Spray paint left by vandals. PHOTO BY CARLETON BERN

[below] Sometimes gates are used to prevent vandals from getting into a cave. PHOTO BY PAUL BURGER

assume the worst. Though they may come off as condescending, they do mean well. Remember that the trip leader would like to be exploring and mapping, too, but has taken a weekend or two to try to help you learn.

PRETRIP PLANNING

Preparation is the key to any cave trip. If you consistently follow a few basic steps, your trips should run smoothly and will be less prone to problems.

IMPORTANT STEPS TO PLANNING A CAVE TRIP

- Establish trip goals.
- Assemble the team.
- Get permission to enter the cave (if applicable).
- Prepare the team.
- Establish a surface watch.

The goals for most training trips are to teach the route through a cave or to some interesting feature, and to teach low-impact caving and basic caving ethics. This type of orientation trip has simple goals—but you still have to prepare.

ORIENTATION PRETRIP CHECKLIST

- The key or combination if the cave is gated.
- A permit or any other type of permission or waiver.
- Permission to enter from landowner or manager.
- A cave map—or preferably one for each team member.
- Emergency contact numbers—the sheriff or a local cave rescue group, for instance.
- Emergency contact numbers for trip members in case of a cave accident.
- A reliable surface watch.

You will need to do more planning for cave mapping, research, and other work trips. If you have been working on a project for a long time, preparation should be easy. You probably have a list of exploration or survey goals already in your head. Make sure the goals are appropriate to the team you have chosen, and make sure you bring all the maps, data, and notes you need to accomplish those goals. The more information you can bring into the cave, the more successful the trip.

ADDITIONAL PRETRIP CHECKLIST FOR MAPPING OR RESEARCH

- Task list.
- List of previously used survey designations.
- Line plot with survey stations.
- Sampling/scientific gear.
- Scientific instruments.
- Also, be sure to gather all your work gear (survey instruments, book, pencils, survey sheets, flagging tape, and so on), and check its condition.

Assembling the Team

Your first step in assembling your team is deciding how many people you need. For a training trip, you do not want too many people. A good ratio is one trip leader or experienced caver for every four newcomers. This will make it easier for you to keep an eye on the entire group and prevent people from getting strung out too far behind. Once you decide on your team size, you can announce the trip at a meeting and pass around a sign-up sheet. Make sure that you have everyone write down their phone number and contact information. You may need to contact them with a list of equipment they need, or to let them know of any changes in the trip. You will also need to establish a meeting place.

For a work trip, you do not want to have more than four people unless you have a large amount of support gear. Extra people on a slow-paced trip will encourage even the most experienced caver to become bored, possibly wander, and cause greater impact on the cave. Choose your team members based on their skills and the type of work you are trying to do.

Landowner or Land Manager Relations

Cavers frequently overlook the importance of maintaining good relationships with landowners or cave managers. Before you and your team arrive, you will need to get permission to enter the cave. Know the access rules before you go. This will keep you from getting fined for trespassing and help keep the cave accessible to those who come after you.

IMPORTANT QUESTIONS TO ASK

How far in advance should I contact the owner for permission?

When should I check in and out with the owner?

What waivers or other paperwork need to be signed?

Does the landowner have any other rules I need to be aware of?

Strive to make a good impression when meeting with the landowner or manager. If you come screeching to a halt in front of the house or office, music blaring and cigarette smoke pouring from the vehicle windows, the owner or manager is less likely to want to give you access. You want to leave the impression that you are safe and responsible. The fastest way to get a cave closed or cause problems for the landowner is to have a cave rescue. All owners worry about liability, and an accident will make them even more hesitant to allow access.

BASIC GUIDELINES FOR PRIVATELY OWNED CAVES

Be courteous.

Leave gates the way you find them.

Do not change clothes in view of the owner's house or roadway.

Do not litter or cause any property damage.

Do not do anything on the owner's property that you would not want done on yours.

Caves managed by state or federal agencies have complex and highly variable access policies. If you aren't familiar with the policies or if it has been a long time since you visited, you need to contact the resource specialist or land manager directly to find out what the policies are. Much of this information is easily available on the Internet. If there are no specific rules or check-in and -out procedures, the following guidelines should help you maintain good land manager relations.

BASIC GUIDELINES FOR GOVERNMENT-MANAGED CAVES

Sign any trail or cave registers placed by the agency.

Do not litter around the caves or deface any signs.

Do not change clothes along roadsides or anyplace where you will be visible by the noncaving public.

Return permits and other paperwork as required.

Do not advertise the cave or publish articles about the cave in the general media without contacting the land manager first.

Following these guidelines for a specific cave or caving project should help you maintain good relationships with landowners or managers. If you prepare well and make sure the team is ready, the trip should go smoothly and successfully.

Preparing the Team

It's your job as trip leader to make sure that everyone on your team is prepared for the caving trip, for the hike to the cave, and, if needed, for camping outside the cave. For beginners, specify the gear each person needs to bring. For experienced cavers, describing the trip and cave should be enough information. This will allow veterans to choose the right clothing, the right pack size, and what equipment they will need.

CAMPING CHECKLIST

- How long is the hike to the cave?
- Will we be backcountry camping, car camping, or staying in a fieldhouse or hotel?
- Will I need to bring a stove, fuel, and cooking gear?
- Is there a good water supply? Do I need a water filter, tablets, and/or bleach?
- What is the predicted weather?
- What is the elevation of the campsite?
- Do I need to pack any group gear to the cave?

CAVING CHECKLIST

- What are the trip goals—slow surveying or fast travel?
- How long will the trip be?
- How wet is the cave?
- How cold is the cave?
- Will there be any climbing or rope-work?
- Will there be long crawls or areas requiring knee and elbow pads?
- Do I need to pack any group gear into the cave?
- Is there any other kind of specialized gear I need—aqua socks, clean clothes for low-impact areas, or the like?

Surface Watches

Now that your caving team is ready, you need to prepare the one team member who will not be going into the cave: your surface watch. This is the person who knows when you are going into the cave, what you plan to do, and when you are supposed to come out. The surface watch will also be the one to send help if you are overdue. You may want to avoid choosing immediate family members of your team, since loved ones are more likely to overreact to late cavers.

QUALITIES OF A GOOD SURFACE WATCH

- Is easily reachable from the time the team goes into the cave to the time the team is expected out and is not going caving during the same time frame.
- Knows the cave well.
- Knows who to contact in case of an emergency and what information to give them.
- Does not panic easily.

Establish a "drop-dead time" when the surface watch will call for help if you are overdue. Choose a reasonable exit time that allows for slower team members, losing track of time, and other factors. A good rule of thumb is to add a third more time to the trip duration than you expect. If you have a very strong team that you know is capable of a long trip, extend your exit time. However, do not set your exit time so late as to make a surface watch pointless. You do not want the response time to be longer than your team could wait in the cave in an emergency such as flooding or serious injury.

More experienced teams with very experienced surface watches can set different levels of response to an overdue team. For example, if a caving team is four hours late, the surface watch can contact the local caving rescue group to let them know to stand by. The surface watch would contact them again after the party has been overdue for eight hours. This would give rescuers a chance to get mobilized quickly if called and prevent them from responding unnecessarily. Such a scaled response will, however, increase the risk of a rescue taking too long to get to the cavers if there is an emergency.

IN-CAVE LEADERSHIP

As trip leader you are responsible for the success of the trip and for the safety of the trip members and cave. You should be prepared for not only the trip you have planned but the unexpected as well. Lead by example; do not take unnecessary risks or try to show off. What you do on a cave trip will have much more influence on others than what you say.

QUALITIES OF A GOOD TRIP LEADER

- Is well prepared and organized.
- Is knowledgeable and open with that knowledge.
- Is flexible and adaptable enough to handle changing cave conditions or changing team dynamics.
- Has good judgment.
- Has the ability and training to handle an emergency.
- Has good caving ethics.
- Is fun to cave with.

Whether you are leading newcomers or experienced cavers, setting a good pace will ensure that everyone has a safe, fun caving trip. Gear the trip toward the team member who is the weakest at any given moment. The caver who is the slowest may change during the trip or with different obstacles. Cavers who move quickly through larger passages or up climbs may be slower in crawlways.

It's not a good idea to put the slowest or weakest team member in the back of the group. Cavers in the front will get to rest while the others move through tight spots or up climbs. Once the last person is past the obstacle, the group will start moving again. This means the person in back won't get a chance to rest. If you have another experienced, strong caver along, put him at the end of the group. This will help the team maintain a good pace and give you a second set of eyes to gauge how the group is doing. As leader, you can adjust the position of the team members to make sure that no one is stuck at the back for the whole trip.

Part of being adaptable and setting the pace is knowing and listening to your team. As the trip leader you are a teacher and should be open to questions and be willing to offer help. Make sure everyone on the team knows it's all right to ask for help or stop the trip. The trip may be too difficult, a team member might be feeling exhausted or ill, or someone may just be having a bad caving day. If you're a beginner, ask other members of your caving club about the leader before you go on a trip. Finding a leader who's a good fit for you will make your transition from beginner to intermediate caver smoother, and you will have much more fun.

Team leaders may change during the course of a trip. The trip leader may guide the team to a specific part of the cave to begin surveying. Once the survey begins, the sketcher becomes the leader of the team, sets the pace, and decides the direction. If you are on a trip that requires technical ropework, the team member with most rigging and vertical caving experience will become the leader to make sure all the equipment is rigged correctly. During research trips, the cave scientist may become the trip leader once the team reaches the study location. In case of an emergency or a rescue, the team member with medical or cave rescue experience may take over.

Though the overall trip leader has the ultimate responsibility for the team, different team members can assume leadership roles depending on the purpose of the trip. This can be confusing to beginning cavers, but is a natural part of trip leadership in caving.

Different Types of Cavers: The Team Member's Perspective

Most team conflicts arise from differences in style among members. As a team member, it's important that you find a leader to fit your style. Leaders fall into four basic types: aggressive, structured, supportive, and coaching.

An *aggressive* leader will go at her own pace and will expect everyone to keep up. This type of leader is good for people who are very confident in their athletic ability and learn skills quickly. Though you will end up more bumped and bruised, you will learn how to cave at a fast, but safe pace. This type of leader is not for those who prefer a slow, more methodical approach.

A *structured* trip leader will check the contents of your pack to make sure you have everything you need. He will plan a series of trips from easy to moderate and will introduce a limited number of new obstacles with each trip. This type of leader is good for those who like to ease into outdoor activities.

A *supportive* trip leader will let the team explore on their own but will watch to make sure that no one gets into trouble or hurt. If someone is having a problem on an obstacle, she will help if asked but otherwise let the person keep trying. If one of the team feels bad about not performing a task well, this type of leader will always provide encouragement. A supportive trip leader is good for those who are confident in their athletic ability and learn best on their own.

A *coaching* leader will provide trips with many obstacles to see how the team does. If someone has a problem, he will talk them through it, giving advice. The coach type will always give team members feedback and make suggestions on everything from caving gear to the best way to tackle an obstacle. This type of trip leader is good for those cavers who like to learn on their own but are willing to take advice in order to get better faster.

Different Types of Cavers: The Leader's Perspective

As a leader, it's crucial that you know the personality of your team. Most cavers are a blend of two or more of the four personality types discussed above. Good leaders can change styles depending on the situation and the team. It's important to recognize these types in your team and yourself so you can anticipate problems and recognize them as conflicts of style, not a battle between you and your team. When you are setting up a team, you can choose like-minded cavers to work with you. When you are leading a training trip, you may be faced with managing several different types of cavers and will have to know how to adapt your style to fit their needs.

Everyone needs to push their limits to get better at caving. If you know the personality of your team members, you will know when and how much to push them. An aggressive caver needs to be pushed and will thrive on the challenge. Cavers who prefer to be coached or supported can be pushed, but only a little. If you push too hard, they may become cranky or belligerent and bring down the morale of the whole team. Pushing too much may also lead to an accident, so it is important to gauge your team correctly.

If you overstructure a group of aggressive cavers, they will become bored and impatient. Aggressive cavers also get annoyed if you try too much coaching; they are content to learn on their own. If you are a supportive or coaching style of caver, try to be more flexible and allow the more aggressive cavers some freedom while staying safe and following the rules of the cave.

Handling personality dynamics is largely an exercise of learning from your mistakes. If you know your style and can quickly recognize the styles of cavers on your team, you will be ahead of the game. The trick is providing a good trip that challenges and satisfies all types. By being flexible and adaptable, you will be able to provide an enjoyable trip and prevent most personality conflicts and other problems.

DEALING WITH COMMON CAVING PROBLEMS

You will encounter fatigue, irritability, rebellious cavers, and personality conflicts while leading or participating on cave trips. You cannot prevent all of these from happening, but knowing how to deal with them will make the rest of the trip more enjoyable for everyone.

BASIC PROBLEM-SOLVING GUIDELINES

- Be patient.
- Be understanding.
- Try to defuse the situation subtly.
- Use direct action only if absolutely necessary.

Fatigue

Fatigue is a physiological problem, not a motivation issue. When your body has used up its energy stores, it cannot function correctly, no matter how motivated you are. Preparation, conditioning, refueling, and setting a reasonable pace are vital to preventing fatigue.

SIGNS OF FATIGUE

- Irritability.
- Sleepiness.
- Poor judgment.
- Weakness.
- Lack of motor coordination.

If one of your team starts exhibiting signs of fatigue, it's time to change the trip. Pushing a fatigued person will lead to accidents and could endanger the whole team. Stop to rest and make sure that the fatigued caver eats and drinks. Encourage the whole team and keep them upbeat, even if you have made the decision to turn the trip around. It is everyone's job to keep up team spirit. Do not spend the rest of the trip complaining about turning back; this will only discourage the person more and bring down the morale of the rest of the team.

A fatigued, irritable caver with diminished judgment may refuse to rest, eat, or drink. Call a group break and encourage everyone else to refuel. Usually the fatigued caver will join in. If you have extra high-energy food, share it with the group and try to get the fatigued person to eat some of your food. Sometimes folks will snack on other people's food when they won't eat their own. Avoid giving an exhausted person candy as an energy boost unless absolutely necessary. Although candy quickly raises the person's blood sugar and apparent energy, it also burns off quickly and leaves the person lower than before.

A fatigued caver may display poor judgment about whether to use handlines on short climbs and may take unnecessary risks. In this case, insist that everyone on the team use a belay. If you do not single out the exhausted person, she is more likely to follow your advice. Move slowly and steadily out of the cave, stopping every half hour or so for breaks and to drink and eat. Always try to maintain a positive attitude and encourage the team.

Place the tired caver near the front of the group and let him set the pace for the whole team. If the person is comfortable with the route and has experience with the obstacles along the route, let him lead out. If not, place a patient, experienced trip leader at the front and make sure she knows to set a pace that is comfortable to the exhausted caver.

Personality Issues

Many personality conflicts can be prevented by knowing the types of cavers you have on your team and adjusting your trip accordingly. There are times, however, when you will not be able to prevent conflicts from happening and will have to deal with them directly.

One of the most common personality problems is irritability. This can be a sign of fatigue, as discussed above; or a caver may just be in a bad mood. The best solution is to stay upbeat and try to keep the rest of the team in good spirits. If you're lucky, the irritable person will snap out of it. Keeping up team morale will prevent one person's mood from infecting the whole group and making the trip miserable.

Conflicts can also arise when one or more of the team wants to go against the rest of the group. There may be instances when a team goes into a cave to survey and one or two people decide they want to explore instead. Or one of the team may want to take a different route through the cave.

If these conflicts occur, first listen to why the renegades do not want to go along with the rest of the team. If a different route is just as reasonable as the one you have chosen, consider taking the alternate route. In some cases you may need to put your ego aside and go with the flow. If you feel that the new route would add too much time to the trip, or think it may not be safe to take everyone through, state those concerns. Most cavers will not want to risk the safety of others just so they can have a good time. You will probably be more successful making these types of arguments than using the old parental adage, "Because I said so."

Of course you cannot completely abandon your work tasks if that is why you have permission to be in the cave. In this case your options as trip leader are limited to either convincing the others to stay on task or turning the trip around. Consider allowing the group to explore ahead and then survey back toward the entrance. This will let them do some exploring and still get the work done. If adjusting the plan slightly does not work, you can use peer pressure. It is rare to have one person willing to mess up everyone else's trip just for the sake of rebellion. There isn't much you can do about this type of caver inside the cave, but you may want to reconsider inviting him on future trips.

Another common problem is very simple: People on your team just don't get along. In the confined spaces of a cave, there is no way for one person to avoid someone else. If you see one person getting on another person's nerves, look at what you can do to defuse the situation.

WAYS TO MITIGATE PERSONALITY CONFLICTS

Separate the people who are in conflict.

Strike up a conversation in order to keep their focus off each other.

If you see one of the team purposely antagonizing another, engage the antagonizer in conversation or give the person a task that will keep him or her too busy to antagonize.

If possible, cut the trip short. These problems will get worse as the team gets more tired.

CAVING RIGHTS AND RESPONSIBILITIES

Finally, I want to leave you with a caving bill of rights and responsibilities. The team leader and team members are equal when it comes to exercising them both.

RESPONSIBILITIES

- To protect your own safety and that of your team.
- To protect the cave and cave environment.
- To follow the rules for the cave and the land you are on.
- To give help when asked or needed.
- To give advice when asked or needed.

RIGHTS

- To stop the trip or turn the trip around.
- To refuse to do anything you believe is unsafe.
- To refuse to do anything you feel would cause harm to the cave.
- To ask for help.
- To ask for advice.

The goal of every caving trip is a safe, fun experience for everyone with the least amount of impact to the cave. A trip is not over until everyone is safely out of the cave, warm, dry, rehydrated, and fed. The most important factor in making the trip successful is good leadership. By following the guidelines in this chapter, your job as trip leader or participant should be much easier.

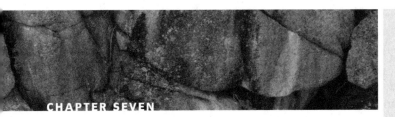

CHAPTER SEVEN

Advanced Caving

VERTICAL CAVING
CAVE CAMPING
ICE CAVES
CAVERN, CAVE, AND
SUMP DIVING

This chapter will give you a brief introduction to several kinds of advanced caving. Each section provides guidance on additional skills, equipment, and training you will need as well as some of the hazards involved. You will need to practice these skills and learn to be extremely comfortable with the techniques before trying any advanced caving.

VERTICAL CAVING

Exploring most of the challenging caves of the world requires ropes. This section will give you only an introduction to vertical caving, but several excellent books are listed in "Additional Resources" at the end of this book; these cover vertical caving in more depth.

KNOWLEDGE AND SKILLS NEEDED FOR VERTICAL CAVING

- The different types of rope.
- Basic knot tying.
- How to tie a harness and etrier out of webbing.
- How to rig a rope and identify good and poor rope rigging.
- How to properly rappel.
- How to use an ascending system.
- How to use proper rope signals.

This section briefly covers the first three topics and provides an overview of what you need to learn for the others. I also outline the basic use of rope signals, since they can be useful on handlines and ladders.

Ropes

You may come across three different types of rope while caving—laid, static kernmantle, and dynamic kernmantle. *Laid rope* is made of three strands of rope twisted together; *kernmantle ropes* have a twisted core with a smooth sheath braided around it. Laid climbing and caving ropes have not been manufactured in many years, so any that you find in a cave are likely to be old and untrustworthy.

Kernmantle ropes can be either static or dynamic. *Dynamic ropes* are designed to stretch so they can absorb the force of a fall. Use dynamic climbing rope when you are free climbing and may fall. *Static rope* is used for most caving situations and is designed to minimize bounce so it will not rub on the edge of a pit and abrade.

BASIC ROPE CARE

Store ropes in a cool, dry place.

Do not leave ropes in the sun; UV light will make them weaker.

Try to keep ropes clean.

Never step on a rope; you can grind dirt into the fibers or break the rope if it's under load.

Replace any rope that someone has taken a fall on.

Replace any rope that has had a lot of use or has been subjected to undue wear (when rigged in a waterfall, for example) for a long time.

Knots

Two of the most common families of knots used in caving are the figure-eight and the bowline. Instead of covering all of them, I will show you several basic knots in the figure-eight family that you can use to rig or tie into a rope, or for emergencies. Practice tying these knots until you can tie them quickly and correctly. I have also included a few basic knots that are used to back up the primary knots. Regardless of which family of knots you prefer, you should be able to tie the knot into the end of the rope, tie the knot on a bight, and tie the knot on a coil.

After you get comfortable tying these knots and those in the bowline family, I recommend learning a few more.

ADVANCED KNOTS

Double figure-eight. Good for rigging to multiple anchors.

Butterfly knot. Good for adding a rig point to the middle of a rope or tying off a bad spot in the rope.

Prusik. Three can be used to ascend a rope.

Munter hitch. This can be used to turn a carabiner into a safe rappel device on short drops or for belaying short climbs.

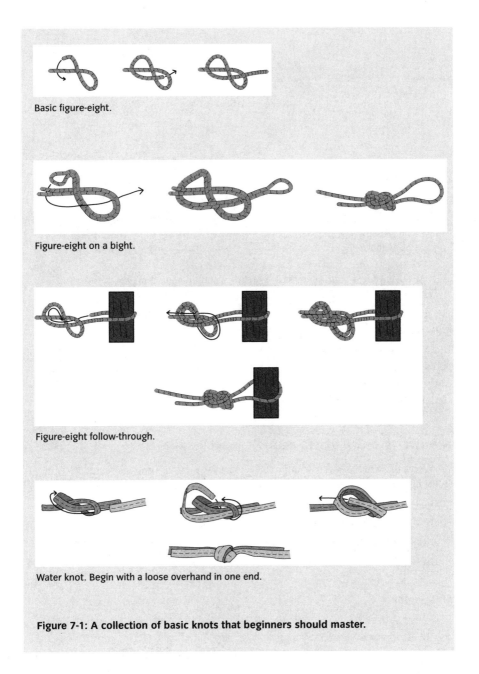

Basic figure-eight.

Figure-eight on a bight.

Figure-eight follow-through.

Water knot. Begin with a loose overhand in one end.

Figure 7-1: A collection of basic knots that beginners should master.

Etriers

An etrier is a length of webbing tied with loops you can put your feet into. It can be very useful for rigging short climbs as well as providing footholds in a narrow fissure.

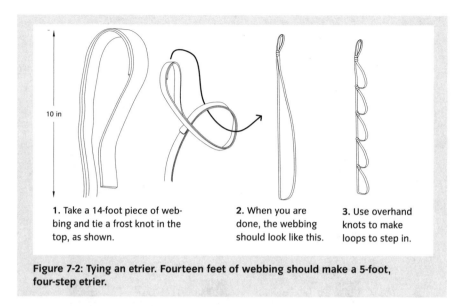

| 1. Take a 14-foot piece of webbing and tie a frost knot in the top, as shown. | 2. When you are done, the webbing should look like this. | 3. Use overhand knots to make loops to step in. |

Figure 7-2: Tying an etrier. Fourteen feet of webbing should make a 5-foot, four-step etrier.

Rigging Ropes

There are two basic types of anchors: natural and artificial. *Natural anchors* can be boulders, bedrock columns, very solid cave formations, or even trees. You can use climbing anchors such as chocks, friends, and cams for rigging in caves, but the most common *artificial anchor* used for caving is a rock bolt.

KNOWLEDGE AND SKILLS REQUIRED FOR RIGGING

- Where to rig the rope to minimize hazards such as waterfalls and rockfalls.
- How to identify and rig good natural anchors.
- How to identify and rig good artificial anchors.
- How to identify improperly placed or worn-out bolts.
- How and when to use rope pads.
- How and when to use rebelays.

Equipment

To explore vertical caves you will need at least a good seat harness, a rappel device, and an ascending system. You can use most climbing harnesses for caving, but many have extra loops for gear that can snag on cave walls. Caving harnesses are specifically designed for use with ascending systems and are better suited to both ascending and rappelling.

Use rappel devices specifically designed for caving. Most climbing rappel devices are not well suited to gritty caving ropes and will not give you the control you will need.

If your local caving club has vertical training classes, you will get the opportunity to try out a number of different devices. Which one you choose depends on how much you weigh, how quickly you like to descend, how frequently you will be carrying a heavy pack, and how much weight you want to carry.

[above] The frog ascending system.
PHOTO BY PAUL BURGER

[right] Typical rappel devices: Petzl Simple, figure-eight, rack. PHOTO BY PAUL BURGER

There are dozens of possible gear combinations that can be used to ascend a rope. The two most common systems are the *ropewalker* and the *frog*. In both systems you are attached to the rope with at least two mechanical ascenders. These ascenders will slide easily up a rope, but have cams that prevent them from slipping back down.

You will need to adjust your gear to your body size, and you'll want to practice in order to become efficient at climbing. Many caving clubs put on vertical caving classes at very little cost—a good way to try out different systems.

KNOWLEDGE AND SKILLS NEEDED FOR RAPPELLING AND ASCENDING ROPES

Basic

How to lock off your descender while on rappel.

How to change from rappelling to ascending while on rope.

How to change from ascending to rappelling while on rope.

How to cross a knot during a rappel or ascent.

How to get upright if your upper ascender or chest harness should fail while climbing.

How to downclimb with your ascenders.

How to properly inspect and maintain your vertical system.

Advanced Rappelling and Ascending Skills

How to use a tether for hauling heavy loads.

How to use your system to climb steep slopes.

How to cross rebelays.

How to assist someone who has inverted.

How to pick off an injured caver from the rope.

How to make field repairs to your gear.

Rope Calls

Even if you aren't planning to learn how to rappel and ascend ropes anytime soon, it's important to know basic rope calls. Use these calls while climbing handlines, rope ladders, and etriers. These calls make it clear what you are doing and when you are ready for the next person to climb up or down.

BASIC ROPE CALLS

"On rope." You are declaring the rope yours and are preparing to climb or descend.

"Climbing." You are on the rope and ascending.

"On rappel." You are on the rope and descending.

"Off rope." You are detached from the rope and clear from the rockfall zone. It's safe for the next caver to get on rope.

When someone is climbing the rock while on a belay, the signals are used a little differently. After the climber has attached himself to the rope and the belayer is secure above, the two might communicate with the following exchange:

CLIMBER: "On belay." Ready to climb.

BELAYER: "Belay on." The belayer is secure and ready to hold the climber if he should take a fall.

CLIMBER: "Climbing." The climber is starting up the rope.

BELAYER: "Climb." Acknowledgment that the climber is starting up.

CLIMBER: "Off belay." The climber has reached the top and is safe from falling back down.

BELAYER: "Belay off." Only now does the belayer let go of the rope and take the climber off belay.

You would use similar calls for rappelling, but would say "rappel" instead of "belay." Consistent use of the same calls on ladders and handlines will make them second nature when you start vertical caving. Clear, concise signals can prevent accidents and will make the trip go more smoothly.

Vertical Caving Hazards

Rockfall is the most common hazard in all caving, but the potential for injury is much greater around pits. You also need to be aware of worn or damaged rope and problems while rappelling or ascending.

ROCKFALL PRECAUTIONS

Clear loose rocks and debris away from the top of a pit where people or the rope could knock debris loose. Even if no one is below you, knocking debris down the pit may loosen rocks farther down. Always yell *"Rock"* when you knock anything down the pit, even if you are sure there is no one below.

Stay out of the rockfall zone at the bottom of the pit. Do not yell "Off rope" until you are out of the rockfall zone.

Rappel and ascend smoothly to minimize rope movement that could loosen rocks.

If you are tethering your pack, be careful not to drag or swing it where it could knock down rocks or break cave formations.

It's worth repeating here that ropes can become worn with use or from the pounding of water. Carefully inspect each rope before rigging it by pinching it in your hand along its length both before and after the cave trip. Look for spots that seem flat, soft, or visibly worn. If any spot on the rope appears to unusually worn, do not use it. Also check the rope anchors to make sure they are solid.

If you learn all the skills described in this section, you should be ready to handle these hazards and begin exploring vertical caves. Take advantage of opportunities to

Getting clothing, hair, or other loose lines jammed in your descender during a rappel.

Rappelling down a rope that is too short to reach the bottom. This is why you always tie a knot on the bottom of the rope before going down.

Carrying a heavy pack on rappel or descent.

Mechanical failure of your climbing system.

Flipping upside down on ascent due to failure of your chest harness or carrying too heavy a pack.

practice with experienced cavers; you will learn more quickly and avoid some of the mistakes most of us made when we began.

CAVE CAMPING

If you are prepared, cave camping can be one of the most enjoyable experiences you'll ever have. If you're not, it can be one of the most miserable. The key is having the right conditioning and the right equipment.

On a typical cave camping trip, you spend one day getting to your camp and setting up your gear. Each day after that, you spend the morning eating breakfast, putting your caving gear together, and setting the tasks for the day. When you make a day trip out of camp, it's much like a normal caving trip, except you don't return to the warmth of the sun—only the dim glow of camp. When you get back to this home base, you change out of caving clothes and into camp clothes, clean up, and cook dinner. During dinner, you go over what your team and the other teams did during the day and set the tasks for the next day. On the last day, you pack up, clean camp, and head for the surface. (Hopefully you remembered to stash sunglasses at the entrance if you are exiting in the daytime.)

KEY POINTS FOR CAVE CAMPING

Cave temperature will determine what types of caving clothes you wear and what you will need to sleep comfortably.

Wet or dry? This tells you what type of pack you will need and how much to waterproof your gear.

Passage size determines how big a pack you can use and how much work it will be getting to camp.

How much work will it take to get to camp—in distance and time?

Water availability will let you know whether you need water purification or filtering, or will need to carry all your water into the cave.

Are there sanitary facilities? This tells you whether you will need room in your pack to haul out waste.

The duration of your stay determines how much food, fuel, clothes, batteries, and so on, you will need to carry.

Typical cave camping gear, including ground cloth, sleeping pad, and synthetic sleeping bag. Across the top (left to right): first-aid kit, water bag, stove, pot, fuel, kitchen kit, and solid waste removal kit.

PHOTO BY PAUL BURGER

BASIC EQUIPMENT FOR CAVE CAMPING

- Larger pack.
- Sleeping gear.
- Different and more food.
- Water treatment.

- Extra first-aid equipment.
- Camp luxuries.
- If you must take regular medication, bring extra doses in case the trip is longer than you expected.

Packs

Cave camping requires much more gear than a normal caving trip, so you will need a bigger pack. We looked at the different types of packs back in chapter 2; review those guidelines to decide what pack you will need. For cave use, do not carry an external-frame pack—these can damage the cave. If you're going to be doing long trips away from camp, you will need a separate caving pack. You can use your camp pack, but since it will be mostly empty, it will be awkward and likely to snag as you move through the cave.

Sleeping Gear

You will need a good lightweight sleeping bag that will keep you warm even if it becomes damp. Down bags have the best weight-to-warmth ratio, but the down absorbs moisture even in a relatively dry cave. A wet down bag will not keep you warm. Choose a synthetic bag with a comfort rating equal to or colder than the cave. In a very warm cave, you may be able to get away with a thinner sleeping bag liner rather than a full sleeping bag.

Bring a groundsheet such as a heavy-duty emergency blanket or piece of plastic to help protect you and your bag from dirt and moisture on the floor. The groundsheet will also collect crumbs and other litter and prevent these from being left in the cave. Be sure to fold the ground cloth with all the debris inside, so you can carry it out of the

A cave camp deep in Jewel Cave, South Dakota. PHOTO BY CARLETON BERN

cave. Use a sleeping pad to keep you insulated from the cold cave floor. If you use an inflatable sleeping pad, make sure to bring a repair kit in case the pad gets a hole during the trip.

Bring a set of dry clothes so you will be comfortable while sleeping or hanging out in camp. I recommend a dry set of thin Capilene tops and bottoms, a pair of wool socks, and a Capilene balaclava. After several days in the cave, you'll really welcome having nice comfortable clothes to wear.

Food

Bring the snack food you normally take on a cave trip for your trips away from camp. You will also need food for breakfast and dinner in camp. Freeze-dried food works the best for conserving weight and packing a lot of calories. Instead of bringing all of the packaging into the cave, open the foil pouches and repack the inner bags into resealable plastic bags or widemouthed bottles. This will reduce the amount of trash you need to carry back out. Then bring either one pot that you can reuse or one of the foil packs to use while you are in camp. If you really want to save space and aren't picky about your food having texture, you can use a blender or coffee grinder to pulverize your food into a much smaller volume. I have found that I can pack more than five freeze-dried packages into a single one-liter, widemouthed bottle.

FOOD AND WATER REQUIREMENTS

- Water purification tablets or water filter.
- Stove and fuel. Bring spare parts for the stove if it has replaceable or user-maintained parts.
- Waterproof matches or lighter.
- A small selection of spices to season bland food. I like to bring a spice mix in a sealed film can.
- Eating utensils. If you bring only one, make it a spoon.
- Vitamin supplements. It is unlikely that the food you bring in will supply all your daily vitamin and mineral needs.

Camp Luxuries

Beyond the basics, there are many items that can make your underground stay more comfortable. You will probably discover a few of your own as you gain experience camping, but these are some I've found particularly useful.

Camping Hazards

Fatigue is the most common hazard on long cave camping trips. With the added weight, you will move slower than you are used to, and it will take more effort. Carrying a camp pack will make you move with all the ease and grace of a pregnant water buffalo. You are more likely to be off-balance and prone to stumbling. The best way to prevent fatigue and stumbling is proper conditioning and setting a comfortable pace.

Caves are a favorable environment for microbes, and there is almost always some kind of crud being passed around. Sanitation tends to be poor and people are in close quarters, so bugs are easily transmitted. If you take vitamin supplements to keep your immune system working well and frequently use hand sanitizers, you can prevent most of these bugs from getting to you—or at least minimize their effects.

ICE CAVES

There are two basic types of ice caves: regular caves that contain some ice, and caves formed completely in ice or snow. Caves with only a small amount of ice merely require limited extra equipment and training. However, if you are exploring a cave that contains steep passages or pits lined with ice, you will need more advanced skills. Although glacier and ice fissure caves are rare in the United States, there are some. You will need very specialized training before exploring this type of cave.

Patches of ice in a Colorado cave. The only specialized gear this situation requires is the nylon suit the caver is wearing to protect against the cold. PHOTO BY CARLETON BERN

ADVANCED ICE SKILLS

Proper use of an ice ax for climbing.

Proper ice ax self-arrest techniques.

Proper use of crampons.

Individual crevasse rescue.

Correct use of ice screws and other methods for rigging ropes into ice.

Identification of safe and unsafe ice conditions.

Caving clubs usually do not teach these skills, but good mountaineering clubs offer courses in ice climbing and crevasse rescue. Remember that areas with ice caves and glaciers may be prone to other high-altitude hazards. I suggest taking courses in winter outdoor skills and avalanche safety to round out your training.

Equipment

To safely explore ice caves, you need the right clothing, the right emergency equipment, and, in some cases, specialized ice gear. The most important equipment decision will be what you wear. Most ice caves are obviously cold and wet, so it's easy to get hypothermia. Wear either clothes that will keep you warm if you get wet or a caving suit that will keep you dry (see chapter 2 for a more complete discussion of clothing types and suggestions). In case of an accident, if someone gets very wet, or if you have to stay longer in the cave than expected, it's also a good idea to bring some emergency gear.

EMERGENCY EQUIPMENT FOR ICE CAVES

An emergency stove to heat water while you're in the cave.

Dry clothing inside the cave.

Emergency clothing, a blanket, or a sleeping bag near the entrance.

To explore some ice caves, you will need specialized tools such as ice axes, crampons, or ice tools. Crampons are metal spikes strapped to your boots that allow you grip on the ice. Ice axes can be used to chop steps in the ice, climb ice slopes, and stop you from sliding down an ice slope. Without proper training, these tools will do you very little good and can become hazards.

Hazards

The main hazards in ice caving are hypothermia, slips and falls, rope damage caused by the sharp edges of ice gear, and falling ice. Frostbite can also be a problem if your boots or other gear are too tight. The most dangerous of these is hypothermia. Dress

Ice axes and crampons are used for exploring ice caves. PHOTO BY PAUL BURGER

appropriately, keep as dry as possible, know the warning signs of hypothermia, and be prepared to treat hypothermia if it occurs.

Ice can be treacherous to walk across, even ice covered with a layer of dirt. You can easily sprain a joint or break a bone slipping on the ice. You can also slip into fissures and get jammed or, worse, fall into a pit. If the cave has only short spans of ice, you may be able to get away with using your normal caving boots. You can rig short handlines for some sections if you come to them from the top. If you need to go up a steep slope, you may need to use crampons or other ice tools to climb safely.

Ice tools such as crampons and ice axes can easily damage rope and can cause serious injury. Proper training will help you learn how to use these tools safely without creating hazardous conditions.

Ice caves are almost as dynamic as river caves, especially during the beginning and late parts of the ice season. Icefalls and sudden bursts of water from the ice are common during these times. Ice is also much easier to break than rock, so it's easy to dislodge large pieces onto cavers below you. Proper training in good and bad ice conditions will help you identify this type of hazard and keep you safe.

CAVERN, CAVE, AND SUMP DIVING

There are three basic types of underwater caving: cavern diving, cave diving, and sump diving. Having an open-water certification or even some advanced open-water training will not prepare you to enter an underwater cave. According to the Cave Diving Section of the National Speleological Society, more than 430 divers have been killed in underwater caves since 1960. Some of these fatalities have included certified open-water scuba instructors.

On a *cavern dive* you will explore only the area of the cave lit by sunlight or less than 300 feet, whichever comes first, and will not go through any constrictions. For this type of dive, you can use regular scuba gear and some additional equipment, but you will still need training. In cavern dive training, you will be taught the basics of the underwater cave environment, some of the hazards, and some of the techniques unique to cave diving.

On a *cave dive* you will explore beyond the cavern zone and will need specialized equipment and training. Cave dive training is broken into three sections: introduction to cave diving, apprentice cave diver, and full cave diver. The introductory course will teach you specialized equipment and skills, but you'll go in only as far as you can reach and exit safely with a single tank of air. The apprentice and full cave diver training provide instruction on advanced cave diving techniques and safety. You need to complete the full training cycle before attempting any complex dive into a cave.

A sump is a water-filled section of an air-filled cave. There are no formal courses for learning to safely dive a sump, but you will need all of the skills required for a cave dive as well as all the skills for dry caving. Most cavern and cave dives are done in relatively clean, warm water in relatively large cave passages. Most *sump dives* are in cold water with poor visibility in smaller passages. Do not attempt a sump dive until you have extensive cave diving practice and are experienced and comfortable with the emergency procedures associated with cave diving.

CAVE DIVING REQUIREMENTS

Skills

Proper use of all specialized caving equipment.

Proper use of guidelines.

Proper emergency procedures.

Proper finning technique to prevent kicking up silt.

Stage diving.

Dive planning.

Equipment

At least three dependable underwater lights.

Diving guideline on a reel.

Submersible pressure gauge.

Backup second stage.

Backup regulator.

Hazards

You will encounter many of the same hazards in underwater caves as you would in air-filled caves, though falling down a pit is not one of them. These caving dangers—compounded by the dangers of scuba diving—make cave diving very risky indeed, especially for the untrained.

The presence of a ceiling is the big difference between open-water diving and cave diving. In an emergency you will not be able to make a free ascent to the surface; you'll have to go back to the entrance. You will need two or three times as much air for a cave dive as an open-water dive.

Getting lost is a hazard in both air-filled and underwater caves. The biggest difference is that in an air cave you can sit and wait for rescue. This is not an option when you are limited by the amount of air you carry. That is why it is imperative that you use a dive line on a reel with dive arrows that point the way out for navigation. This dive line can also become a hazard if you don't know how to use it properly. There have been many cave diving fatalities caused by an inexperienced diver getting tangled in the line.

Open-water divers frequently overlook one of the most dangerous hazards in cave diving: silt. Normal open-water swimming techniques easily stir up the fine silt that settles on the floors of cave passages. Imagine you are swimming along in a nice, clear cave passage and turn around to see a thick cloud of silt blocking your way. Without a dive line, it will be impossible for you to find your way out. Without the proper training, even a guideline may not allow you to reach the entrance safely.

Without specialized training, experience, and equipment, you likely won't survive diving into an underwater cave. You will also risk the lives of the rescue or recovery divers who have to come in to find you.

The purpose of this chapter has been to give you some basic direction on what kinds of skills, training, and equipment you will need for doing more advanced caving. These guidelines are not intended to be a substitute for additional training and practice. You will find additional resources for many types of advanced caving at the back of this book.

Glossary of Caving Terms

Anchor: A solid object such as a tree, rock, or bedrock wall that a rope can be tied or attached to.

Bad air: Air that is either low in oxygen or high in nonbreathable gases such as methane or carbon dioxide.

Balaclava: A hood that covers the entire head with an opening for the face, usually made of wool or synthetic material.

Belay: A safety line used by one caver to help another keep from falling in case of a slip. Also, the act of providing a safety line for another caver.

Bolt: A metal pin driven into the rock so that a hanger can be attached to fix a rope to solid rock.

Boulder cave: A cave that is essentially the spaces between fallen rock. Also known as a talus cave.

Breakdown: Large blocks of fallen rock in a cave. These rocks generally fall when a cave is first drained of water or as surface streams intersect the cave.

Calcite: A pure crystalline form of calcium carbonate, the primary component of limestone.

Canal: A narrow stream or river passage with a swift current and solid bedrock walls.

Chimney: A climb narrow enough to bridge across in order to go up or down. Also, the act of climbing a chimney.

Cowstail: A length of rope or webbing used to attach a seat harness to a rope, ascender, or bolt while doing vertical or technical caving.

Duck-under: A place in a dry passage where you have to lower your head to get through. Also, a short section of submerged cave passage where you can hold your breath and quickly get through.

Dynamic rope: Nylon rope designed to stretch in order to absorb the shock of a fall.

Epigenic cave: A cave formed by the action of surface waters descending into the ground and dissolving rock.

Etrier: A simple ladder made of webbing or rope with loops to put your hands and feet into.

Flowstone: An area where water has flowed across a wide area and deposited thin layers of calcite to resemble a frozen waterfall or smooth surface.

Formations: Cave decorations such as stalactites, stalagmites, columns, and flowstone. Also called speleothems.

Free climb: A climb that does not require rope to ascend or descend. Also, the act of climbing without rope.

Guano: Bat or bird droppings.

Gypsum: A soft mineral made of calcium sulfate that can form speleothems such as flowers and needles.

Handline: Rope or webbing used to assist a caver up or down a climb without technical ascending or descending devices.

Harness: A belt with attached leg loops used to support a caver while attached to a rope.

Helictite: A speleothem that twists or curls as it grows, making it look like a worm or snake.

Hypogenic cave: A cave formed by water rising up from below and dissolving the rock, usually as the result of two different kinds of water mixing together.

Hypothermia: A reduction of body core temperature more than two degrees. Also called exposure.

Joint-controlled cave: A cave formed along well-defined cracks or fractures in the bedrock.

Karst: A landscape characterized by poor surface drainage, caves, sinkholes, and springs.

Lava tube: A cave formed by cooling lava as it flows away from a volcanic vent.

Limestone: A rock made primarily of calcium carbonate and usually formed around oceans or seas by living organisms.

Maze cave: A complex cave consisting of multiple levels and/or intersecting passages that make it difficult to navigate through without getting confused.

Popcorn: A knobby speleothem formed by evaporation of water from cave walls or caused by water splashing off the floor or a stalagmite.

Pothole: A hole large enough to step into that's carved into the floor of a stream passage by water.

Rappel: A pit that requires a rope and technical descending equipment to go down. Also, the act of descending a pit on rope.

Rebelay: An anchor or other rigging point used to redirect a rope away from waterfalls, sharp edges, or other obstacles. Also, the act of redirecting the rope.

Rigging: The combination of ropes, bolts, and webbing used to anchor or redirect a rope for descent or ascent. Also, the act of anchoring a rope for descent and ascent.

Rimstone dam: A speleothem caused by the slow buildup of calcium carbonate at the downstream end of a shallow pool.

Sinkhole: A surface depression where water enters the subsurface in karst areas, or a depression caused by the collapse of an underlying cave passage.

Speleothem: Cave decorations such as stalactites, stalagmites, columns, and flowstone. Also called formations.

Squeeze: A cave passage just large enough to fit through.

Stalactite: A speleothem that grows downward from the ceiling like an icicle via the slow accumulation of minerals such as calcium carbonate.

Stalagmite: A speleothem that grows upward from the floor via the slow accumulation of minerals such as calcium carbonate.

Static rope: Nylon rope designed with very little stretch in order to minimize bouncing when used as a fixed line in vertical drops.

Sump: A place where the cave passage is completely filled with water.

Troglobite: Cave dwellers that are adapted to and complete their life cycle in the total darkness of a cave.

Troglophile: Animals that prefer environments like caves but can survive outside if suitable habitat exists.

Trogloxene: Animals that frequently use caves but must return to the surface for food or other needs.

Tyrolean traverse: A traverse along or across an obstacle that is rigged with a rope anchored tightly between two points so that you hang directly on the rope.

Additional Resources

ADDITIONAL READING

Advanced Techniques and First Aid

Alpine Caving Techniques by Georges Marbach and Bernard Tourte, translated into English by Melanie Alspaugh. Speleo Projects, 2002. An excellent guide to European-style caving with good sections on technical rigging of waterfalls and stream passages.

On Rope: North American Vertical Rope Techniques, 2nd edition, by Alan Padgett and Bruce Smith. National Speleological Society, 1997. An excellent reference on American single-rope techniques, including rigging and vertical systems.

On Call: A Complete Reference for Cave Rescue, edited by John Hempel and Annette Fregeau-Conover. National Speleological Society, 2001. A reference manual on North American cave rescue techniques.

The American Red Cross First Aid and Safety Handbook by Kathleen A. Handal. Little, Brown, 1992.

NOLS Wilderness First Aid, 3rd edition, by Todd Schimelpfenig, Linda Lindsey, and Joan Safford. Stackpole Books, 2000.

Knots for Climbers, 2nd edition (How to Climb Series), by Craig Luebben. Falcon Press, 2001.

Basic Rockcraft by Royal Robbins. LA Siesta Press, 1970. The classic knot reference.

On Station by George R. Dasher. National Speleological Society, 1997. An excellent reference on surveying caves and drawing maps.

Biology

Dark Life: Martian Nanobacteria, Rock-Eating Cave Bugs, and Other Extreme Organisms of Inner Earth and Outer Space by Michael Ray Taylor. Scribner, 1999. This popular book talks about the search for cancer cures and microbes in caves.

Geology and Speleology

Cave Minerals of the World, 2nd edition, by Carol Hill. National Speleological Society, 1997. An illustrated guide to minerals and speleothems found in caves.

Speleology: Caves and the Cave Environment by George W. Moore, G. Nicholas Sullivan, and Nicholas Sullivan. Cave Books, 1997. An excellent reference on basic cave science.

Cave Conservation

Living with Karst: A Fragile Foundation by George Veni, Harvey DuChene, Nicholas C. Crawford, Christopher G. Groves, George N. Huppert, Ernst H. Kastning, Rick Olson, and Betty J. Wheeler. American Geological Institute, 2001. A very nice circular describing caves and karst systems in simple terms.

Cave Conservation and Restoration, edited by Val Hildreth Werker and Jim C. Werker. National Speleological Society, 2005. A handbook on low-impact caving techniques and methods to protect and restore caves.

Leave No Trace: Outdoor Skills and Ethics, Caving by Liz Tuohy. National Outdoor Leadership School, 2000. A nice booklet covering the basics of low-impact caving.

LOCAL AND NATIONAL CAVING CONTACTS

National Speleological Society
2813 Cave Avenue
Huntsville, AL 35810-4431
www.caves.org
For information on caving groups in your area: www.caves.org/info

American Cave Conservation
Association
119 East Main Street
P.O. Box 409
Horse Cave, KY 42749
www.cavern.org/acca/accahome

Project Underground
6245 University Park Drive, Suite B
Radford, VA 24141
www.dcr.state.va.us/underground

SPECIALTY CAVING GEAR

Bob and Bob
P.O. Box 441-W
Lewisburg, WV 24901
www.4bobandbob.com

Inner Mountain Outfitters
41 Herald Drive
Bethlehem, GA 30620
www.caves.org/imo

Karst Sports
Route 1, Box 184
Shinnston, WV 26431
www.karstsports.com

On Rope 1
5490-C Highway 58
Harrison, TN 37341
www.onrope1.com

SPECIALTY CAVING BOOKSELLERS

National Speleological Society
Bookstore
2813 Cave Avenue
Huntsville, AL 35810-4431
www.caves.org/service/bookstore

Speleobooks
P.O. Box 10
Schoharie, NY 12157-0010
www.speleobooks.com

Speleoprojects (Switzerland)
www.speleoprojects.com

Index

About the Author

Paul Burger began caving in 1985 as a high school student involved with the Colorado Springs Parks and Recreation Department. Most of his early caving involved exploring and mapping caves in Colorado and New Mexico, most notably Lechuguilla Cave in Carlsbad Caverns National Park. His continued exploration and mapping in Lechuguilla Cave helped to make it one of the longest caves in the world at over 115 miles and the deepest limestone cave in the United States.

Paul was instrumental in the discovery of Southern Comfort, a major extension to Wind Cave, South Dakota, and has been involved in the exploration of a major new extension to Jewel Cave, South Dakota.

After finishing both his bachelor's and master's degrees in geology at the Colorado School of Mines, Paul went to work for Carlsbad Caverns National Park where he currently serves as the park geologist-hydrologist. He continues to be involved in Lechuguilla Cave exploration and has recently been a part of several international caving expeditions to Mexico and China. Paul also co-authored *Deep Secrets,* a book on the discovery and early exploration of Lechuguilla Cave.